Deep Waters

Insights into the Five Books of Moses and the Jewish Festivals

by

Rabbi Arnie Singer

Deep Waters
Second Edition
Copyright © 2007 by Arnold Singer
All rights reserved.
This book may not be reproduced in whole or in
part, by any means, without permission.

Rabbi Arnie Singer
arnie.singer@gmail.com
www.arniesinger.com
212-663-9550

To my loving parents,
Marc and Jeane Singer
For giving me the gift of a Jewish education.

To Natalie,
For giving me the strength and encouragement
To continue growing.

ACKNOWLEDGEMENTS

Thanks to my colleagues at the Manhattan Jewish Experience, R. Mark Wildes, R. Jonathan Feldman, and R. Ezra Cohen, for giving me the opportunity to inspire.

Thanks to my congregants, students, and friends at MJE for their support and encouragement.

Thanks to all of my holy rabbis who transmitted their Torah wisdom to me. They would not, out of humbleness, want me to list their names here and I would not want to embarrass them if some of my ideas do not meet their standards. I am forever their humble student.

Thanks to Michal Cohen for contributing her design and layout skills.

Thanks to Devorah and Phillipe Benedict and family (especially Rachelle) for always inspiring me at their Shabbat table and for their warmth and caring. They are family to me.

Table of Contents

SERMONS

Rabbi Arnie Singer

INTRODUCTION

Torah is the Hebrew word used to describe the Five Books of Moses, known to the Christian world as the Old Testament. The *Torah* was given to the Jewish People by God at Mount Sinai and throughout their forty years of wandering in the wilderness. It is not a history book, although it contains historical material. It is not a book of stories, although it contains some of the greatest stories ever told. It is the communication of the will of God, and the guide to attaining closeness to the Divine.

Some of the basic principles of the *Torah* apply to all mankind, while the majority, including the hundreds of commandments relating to the details of life and death, apply specifically to the Jewish People. This doesn't mean that the Jews possess the only way of reaching that state of spiritual bliss for the soul called "Heaven". Every person, by following the basic laws of moral conduct, can attain a place in Heaven. The various monotheistic religions each have their own path. The *Torah* is the unique, and often challenging, path for the Jew. Only through the teachings of the *Torah* can a Jew fulfill his spiritual destiny.

Since the giving of the *Torah*, accompanied by orally transmitted interpretations and teachings, over 3500 years ago, the Jews have relentlessly studied, analyzed, and questioned it in order to understand its true meaning. Since the *Torah* is the word of God, it is as relevant today as it was three millennia ago. It is our constant challenge to uncover the relevancy of the *Torah* and apply its lessons to our own lives.

In *Deep Waters* I have tried to apply the ancient messages of the *Torah* to modern life. The *Torah* is divided into fifty two portions called "*Parsha*(s)", one of which is read every Sabbath of the year in the Synagogue. The *Parsha* of the week is usually studied in the order of its reading. The first section of this book is devoted to the study of the weekly *Parsha*. The chapters are divided according to the weekly *Parsha*. Some chapters have more than one lesson. Many of the lessons are followed by personal reflections. Not every *Parsha* is included in this work. The second section of this book is

Deep Waters

devoted to the Jewish holidays, fast days, and commemorative events. The final section includes sermons that I delivered at the Manhattan Jewish Experience.

Almost all of the ideas presented in this book are my own, based on the *Torah* that I have learned over the decades from my holy teachers, who I will not name here for fear of embarrassing them. I did not identify the specific Midrashic, Talmudic, Rabbinic, or Chassidic sources cited, in an attempt to keep this work user friendly and easy to read. I cited the sources of the teachings that I transmitted in their entirety, at the beginning of the respective lesson. All of the lessons in *Deep Water* were written to stand independently of each other, and therefore, some ideas are repeated. I used the third person masculine "he" or "him" throughout the book for simplicity and uniformity.

I hope that this work will bring the *Torah* to life, and demonstrate how the lessons and teachings within it can help us lead more fulfilling lives.

The Book

of

Bereshit

"Creation"

BERESHIT – *Step by Step*

According to many rabbinic opinions, the six days of creation are not meant to be understood as twenty four hour time periods. The most obvious proof to this is that the sun and moon, which determine day and night, were only created on day three. The days of creation must therefore be understood either as some unknown unit of time, or simply as an educational vehicle used by God to teach us life lessons.

The most basic tenet of Judaism is that God is all powerful or omnipotent. Why then did God create the world in six "days" instead of just one? The reason is to teach us that creation is a step by step process. It doesn't all happen at once.

We live in an age of instant gratification. We keep cell phones with us at all times to make sure that we never fall out of instant contact. The speed of our internet connections and computers must constantly be improved to be useful. We demand nothing less than immediate fulfillment of our online orders. We join gyms and follow specialty diets expecting to see immediate results. We often get excited about a new project and dive in with all our energy only to lose steam if it takes a bit longer than expected.

The first thing God teaches us in the Torah is that creating something is a process that takes time and patience.

Reflections

Make a list of your goals and objectives, to be accomplished within an expected time frame. Take another look at the time frame. Is it realistic?

If you've set aside a realistic length of time, be aware that there will be periods when you will lose interest or become discouraged. It is during these periods that most people quit.

When you start a new business you need to have enough capital not only to get started, but also to keep you going through the difficult start up period during which you probably will not be making money. This is true with any project or objective you engage in. You need to amass enough positive spiritual and emotional energy to carry you through those inevitable discouraging and depressing times.

Every step required to reach an objective is usually not equally satisfying. Some steps are tedious and mundane. It's important to realize that those steps are necessary to reach the final objective and therefore, must be taken with the same care and diligence as the enjoyable ones.

Relationships are a good example. They often start off with excitement and infatuation but then usually settle into a more predictable and ordinary pattern. If the relationship is important to you and you want it to succeed you need to remain enthusiastic and actively involved all the time. Creating anything worthwhile takes patience, commitment, and faith in the outcome.

BERESHIT – *Let There Be Light*

There is no event more dramatic and significant than the creation of the world. However, the actual description of creation found in the initial verses of Genesis is anything but dramatic. The first Divine act of creation is described in one brief sentence, "*Vayomer Elokim Yihee Or, Vayihee Or* - And God said let there be light, and there was light". No fireworks, earthquakes, explosions, or cosmic upheavals. Just two words, "*Vayihee Or* – Let there be light". As soon as God said, "let there be light", there was light. The usage of the verb form "*Yihee* – let there be" and "*Vayihee* – and there was" is repeated in the description of the creation of the sky and of the solar and lunar luminaries.

This anti climactic description of the creation of light, as well as the other heavenly objects, teaches us an important lesson. How does one create light in one's life? There is nothing to buy, build, assemble, or borrow. To bring light into your life all you need to do is to say that it's already there. Whether we view our lives and the world around us as filled with light or with darkness is totally up to us. The same event can be seen as positive or negative depending on our perspective. If we want light in our life all we need to do is change our perspective and say, "let there be light". As soon as we proclaim there to be light, there will be.

BERESHIT - *It Was Good*

A famous rule of traditional biblical exegeses is that the first incidence of any word in the bible defines its meaning and character. This *Parsha* of *Bereshit* (Genesis) introduces the concepts of good and bad. The Hebrew for good is *Tov* and for bad is *Lo Tov*. To define the essence o f *Tov* and *Lo Tov* we must follow our rule and find their initial appearances in the *Torah*.

The first time *Tov* is used is when God sees that the light He created is *Tov*. Therefore, the essence of Goodness (*Tov*) is light and all that it represents in the spiritual and mystical realms, i.e. expansiveness, illumination, clarity, uplifting etc. The first *Lo Tov* is found in the verse where God says, "It is bad (*Lo Tov*) for Man to be alone". Therefore, according to our rule, the essence of "bad" is loneliness. Everything bad in the world stems from Man's loneliness.

We can understand this in a couple of ways. Man's absolute physical loneliness leads to the extinction of the human race and, with it, the entire purpose of God's creation. Also, Man's isolation undermines the concept of community, without which civilization cannot grow and flourish.

On a deeper level, loneliness is not just a physical condition. A person can be amongst crowds of people and still be lonely. Loneliness is a state of mind that prevents a person from opening up to others. It is a condition that leads a person to think that no one else is good enough to understand him or to share in his joy or pain. It prevents a person from loving, because love is really the opposite of loneliness. Love is giving oneself so completely to another that one's own soul is bound forever with them. The *Torah* teaches us that without love the "*Tov*" of God's magnificent creation becomes "*Lo Tov*".

The battle between good and evil is really a battle between loneliness and selfishness, and love and selflessness. Light and Good (*Tov*) is victorious when we join with friends and family in a loving and caring unit and the Not Good (*Lo Tov*) prevails when we isolate ourselves in a narrow, selfish, and self centered existence. Let's strive for *Tov*.

BERESHIT - *Where Are You?*

In this *Parsha* Adam and Eve transgress the single rule given to them by God by eating from the tree forbidden to them. Since there was only one prohibition in existence it was as if they had committed every possible sin. They were guilty of as much as was humanly possible at that moment. They hit rock bottom. The *Torah* then tells us that they heard the voice of God traveling through the Garden, but it attaches no words to this voice. Then God calls out to Adam with one word -- "*Ayeko*" or "where are you?" It is the only time that that particular word is used in the bible. Adam tries to hide from God but is finally forced to face Him and respond. He responds by blaming Eve, instead of admitting his mistake and repenting for it. According to the Sages Adam is punished more for his response than for his actual transgression.

Everyone hits a point in their life when they feel like they've hit rock bottom. Events and circumstances take control and it feels as though there is no way out. Hopelessness and despair take over. Suddenly, you hear a voice. There are no words; just a powerful feeling that something with your life is not right. Something inside of you begins to yearn for a change, but it's still too weak to overpower your situation. Then you hear that powerful question, "where are you?" Where am I? What am I doing with my life? Am I fulfilling my potential? Am I fulfilling the deepest desires of my soul? Am I happy?

How do you answer that question, "where are you?" Do you try to avoid it by running away from it, hiding in excuse,s and blaming circumstances and people for your actions? Or do you admit your mistakes and try to change?

The story of Adam and Eve provides us with a guide to follow.

NOAH – *Great or Mediocre?*

The *Torah* describes Noah as *Tzadik*, or righteous man, but qualifies that description by adding the words "in his generation". The Rabbis of the *Midrash* are split as to whether he was righteous solely relative to the evil in his own generation or whether he would also be called righteous had he lived in the generation of Abraham. Why do the Rabbis need to denigrate Noah? Why not just let him by remembered simply as a "*Tzadik*" without qualification?

One of the reasons given in defense of the denigration is as follows. When Abraham was faced with witnessing the destruction of the evil city of Sodom he argued and pleaded with God to spare the city. When Noah was faced with the destruction of the entire world he didn't argue, plead, or pray for it. He just focused on saving his immediate family and the animals that God commanded him to save. Noah had the opportunity to be even greater than Abraham but he failed to reach out to his fellow man. The Rabbis teach us to respect the integrity of Noah but to follow the path of Abraham by reaching out to, protecting, and fighting for those less fortunate or in need.

Some commentators explain that what appears to be a denigrating comment against Noah by the Rabbis is in fact an indirect way of praising him. One of the great Hasidic masters teaches, based on the *Zohar*, that when a *Tzadik* rebukes the evil doers of his generation and they refuse to listen, he acquires their "good portion". Therefore, by living in an evil generation Noah was able to achieve greater merit and righteousness than had he lived at another time.

I think one possible way of understanding this teaching is as follows. Often, when surrounded by people who are hostile to a person's beliefs, that person will fortify themselves in those beliefs to an even greater degree. It is not uncommon for a Jew living in a place devoid of, or hostile to, Judaism to feel an increased sense of urgency and passion to observe Jewish rituals. In the darkest days of the Nazi death camps Jews risked their lives to perform the smallest acts of observance to demonstrate their resolve and fortitude in the face of their oppressors. A

Jew living in suburban Indiana might wake up early and regularly walk for miles to a Synagogue on *Shabbat*, all the while feeling passionate

about his commitment to his heritage. However, that same Jew living in a comfortable Jewish neighborhood with synagogues only blocks away might sleep late and get to Synagogue in time for the Kiddush, if at all.

Noah was a *Tzadik* and would have remained one even in the generation of Abraham. However, surrounded by an evil generation hostile to everything he believed in, Noah became an even greater *Tzadik* than he could ever have become in the generation of Abraham.

Reflections

Intentionally placing ourselves in a challenging environment is not recommended, for we can't be certain that we will succeed. The goal is to remain enthusiastic and passionate, in a challenge free situation.

NOACH – *Societal Breakdown*

In this *Parsha* the *Torah* describes the degeneration of the world in the days of Noah. The *Midrash* explains that this degeneration was the result of three areas of sin: sexual immorality, idolatry, and robbery. Immediately following this description the verse states that God saw the deterioration of civilization resulting from robbery and decided to destroy it. Based on this verse, the fact that there was rampant sexual immorality and idolatry didn't provoke God's destruction of the world. Rather, it was just robbery. Why the overwhelming emphasis on robbery as the cause of the world's destruction?

Although the sins of sexual immorality and idolatry are cardinal, they are offenses solely against God. These sins essentially cause no intentional harm to man. As despicable as they may be, they often serve to bring men closer, even if for sinister purpose. Robbery, however, represents a physical attack by one man against another. It is the result of hatred, jealousy, and anger. It drives men apart and tears apart societal order.

We are all, so to speak, God's children. When God, the "parent", sees his children living together in peace He feels a sense of pride and is willing to overlook their transgressions against Him. However, when He sees his children fighting against one another, He does not turn away and ignore it.

When God saw rampant robbery in the world He recognized that Mankind had used its freedom to choose a path leading to the destruction of civilization. It was disrespect and hatred between men that caused them to forfeit their right to exist in God's world.

The lesson is blatant. God can forgive Man's attempt to sin against Him. He does not forgive Man's attempt to harm his fellow man. Only Man can do that.

NOAH - *The Right Path*

In this *Parsha* of Noah the *Torah* explores two different reactions of Man to the challenges of civilization.

When Noah is faced with a society degenerated to the point of total breakdown his reaction is to isolate himself. In fact, although he is referred to in the opening verses of the *Torah* portion as a *Tzadik*, righteous person, the Rabbinic commentators castigate Noah for not reaching out to his fellow citizens in an attempt to save them from their prophesized destruction. Noah builds for himself a Teyva, which is commonly translated as an Ark. The literal translation for Teyva is actually "box". Instead of building a "boat" with which to save as much of society as possible Noah builds a "box" for himself and his immediate family. The "Noah Model" of dealing with society is isolationism or living inside of a box.

Later in the *Parsha* the *Torah* describes a society striving for complete unity at the expense of the identity of its individual members. Its objective was the total assimilation of its members into one homogeneous entity with a single language, culture, belief system, and personality. This society was called Bavel by the *Torah*. Bavel means totally assimilated or "melting pot". The "Bavel Model" of dealing with society is assimilation to the extent of totally negating the individual to achieve societal uniformity. This model failed disastrously.

It is only with the introduction of Abraham that the *Torah* finally gives us the successful model of how to interact with society. The "Abraham Model" takes the middle path between the Noah and Bavel extremes. Abraham is not afraid to stand up against a world of idolatry in his solitary belief in God (his "box") yet he is also not afraid to interact with that world to try and share his ideas with it. The "Abraham Model" teaches us to be as powerful as a fortress in our beliefs and ideals and to be confident enough to interact with general society without the fear of losing our own identity. By following this path Abraham was able to change the world in an amazing way, something Noah and Bavel could not.

Reflections

It is often easier to take the extreme path. Being in the "middle" is difficult because it forces us to constantly evaluate whether to accept or reject outside influences. Taking the middle path requires the knowledge with which to evaluate other ideas, and the fortitude to make honest decisions and to live by them. It is also the most rewarding path when undertaken successfully, because it allows us to enjoy the best of both worlds.

LECH LECHA – *Lessons of Faith*

Our patriarch Abraham is introduced into a world dominated by idolatry and spiritual darkness where only a few individuals are even aware of the existence of God. Abraham discovers God on his own, either as a child of five or at the age of forty. For the greater part of his life Abraham leads a lonely life of faith, with no one to share his spiritual challenges, other than his wife Sarah.

The Sages in the Talmud emphasize this point in their explanation of the appendage of "Ivri" to Abraham's name. Ivri is commonly translated as Hebrew, however, the word also means "other side". The Rabbis explain that Abraham was on one side, with his faith in God, and the rest of the world was on the other side, with their idolatry.

Imagine the loneliness without a community of likeminded people and the likely pressure exerted upon him to join the rest of the world. But Abraham stood firm against the pressure and enticements of the pagan world and remained true to his beliefs without any reinforcement other than his simple faith in God.

The first time Abraham received any confirmation of his beliefs was at age seventy five when God revealed Himself to him with the terse prophecy commanding him to leave Haran for Canaan. After all those decades of loneliness and struggle, his faith was finally validated.

There are two important lessons to be learned from this. We often feel that our faith goes unverified and our prayers unanswered. We fail to see the hand of God in the world and fall into the trap of thinking that God really does not play a role in our lives. We can learn from Abraham how to remain firm in our faith against even the greatest odds and that, often, matters of faith only become clear when we have enough years to see things from a broader perspective.

Abraham first embarked on his divinely ordained mission at the age of seventy five, when most of his peers were undoubtedly engaged in the pursuits of the retired. He was probably tired from a lifetime of struggle, and would have been extremely satisfied to spend his golden years resting and relaxing. Instead, Abraham jumped at the opportunity to accomplish the mission given to him by God by embarking on a new chapter of his life, starting over in a foreign land, and dealing with the inevitable challenges associated with such an endeavor.

It's never too late to fulfill your destiny, even if it means leaving everything behind and starting from scratch.

Reflections

Some think that a person has a productive period of their life in which to accomplish their goals and fulfill their dreams. This period is usually in their youth and early middle age. Once that time has past it's over! You missed your chance. Abraham showed us that this way of thinking is wrong. Every moment of life is valuable. We can accomplish great things at any age.

ABRAHAM – *Forcing the Hand of God*

Abraham's patriarchal journey officially begins with God commanding him to go to the land of Canaan. This one brief command compels Abraham to uproot his entire life in a dramatic show of absolute faith in, and obedience to, his God. The drama and intensity of this act of faith is slightly dampened, however, when we study the verses preceding it and find that Abraham had set off on his journey to Canaan, with his father Terach, decades before receiving any Divine command. If Abraham was going there anyway why was God's command to him so momentous?

The *Zohar* teaches that things happen in the Heavens only as a result of things that happen in the world. Man must act first and awaken the graces of heaven. Miracles can happen if Man induces them with his actions.

Abraham is a prime example of Man taking the first step to induce a heavenly response. Abraham was spiritually sensitive to the degree that he was able to instinctively sense that the land of Canaan (Israel) was a place containing great holiness and spiritual energy. He, therefore, immediately convinced his family to journey there. His actions showed his enthusiasm and dedication to the pursuit of spirituality, thereby arousing the graces of heaven, leading to God's command to him.

Abraham continues to spur the heavens to action by aggressively pursuing interactions with the Divine. He bargains with God for the lives of the inhabitants of Sodom until he succeeds in at least saving Lot and his family. He sits outside of his tent waiting for God to send him guests until God finally speaks to him and sends him angels disguised as men. He enthusiastically attempts to follow God's command for him to sacrifice his only son, by awaking early in the morning and making his preparations to be able to begin his journey as soon as possible. These are only a few examples that illustrate Abraham's ability and willingness to rouse the heavens with his actions.

Abraham is chosen to be the father of the Jewish people precisely because of this. God wants Man to "provoke" Him into acting on his behalf by displaying faith in Him. Man can awaken the heavens and thereby merit the greatest miracles and salvations.

ABRAHAM — *True Nature*

The *Midrash*, as cited by Rashi, explains the words, "*Lech Lecha* - Go for your sake", to imply that only there, in the Land, will "your nature be made known in the world".

Man's true nature, encompassing his true potential, is usually hidden until it is revealed under the right setting in the right environment. This setting and environment is vital to the fulfillment of Man's full potential. Under the wrong circumstances in the wrong environment that same person might never achieve his full potential, although he might seem outwardly successful.

As great and spiritually developed as Abraham was, he could never reach his complete potential outside of the Land of Israel.

Reflections

Our environment and the people that we associate with influence us and effect our growth. The Sages stress the importance of neighbors, since they can influence our actions for the good or bad. We need to break away from relationships that we see are holding back our growth. We also need to make sure we choose our friends and neighbors with great care.

VAYERA - *Isn't One Enough*

In this *Parsha* Abraham pleads with God to spare the city of Sodom from destruction. He is so brazen as to actually bargain with God. He begins by asking God to spare the city if there are fifty righteous inhabitants dwelling therein, and continues lowering the number until reaching ten. God agrees to spare Sodom if there are just ten righteous people living there. At this point Abraham quits his pleading and accepts God's final offer, sealing the fate of the city for destruction, except for his nephew Lot and Lot's family whom God promises to rescue.

Why didn't Abraham continue pleading with God to save Sodom for the sake of fewer than ten people? Doesn't Judaism teach that every single person is holy and that saving one person is equivalent to saving the entire world?

According to Jewish tradition ten people constitute a community with all of the powers that come with that status. One of the powers of a community is its ability to cry out to God as one and be heard more readily than an individual in the same situation. We find the most glaring example of this during the confession service on the High Holidays. When recited by the individual in private prayer the confession is recited submissively in muted tones. However, when recited by the congregation as one community, that same confession is sung loudly to a joyous and triumphant melody. This is because our Rabbis teach that as a community we have a "direct line" to God and God's promise to hear our prayers and have mercy on us.

As righteous as a person is, his voice will eventually be overpowered and drowned out by evil if it remains isolated and alone. The Kabbalah teaches that when evil is given the power to reign, the individual righteous are overpowered by it as well. This is why Lot and his family were commanded not to look back while fleeing from Sodom. By looking back they would be connecting themselves to the evil community there, thereby subjecting themselves to that community's fate. Abraham realized that without a community even the individual righteous people in Sodom would have no hope of remaining righteous and surviving in such a sea of evil. Therefore, he stopped bargaining at ten. The righteous individuals would have to completely sever their connection with the evil, and flee to survive.

Reflections

Even though we need to live our lives and hold on to our values and heritage in a society which is probably not totally righteous, we also must realize that we can't survive solely on our own. We need to join together as a community to grow. We need to be among other people who practice our values and share our heritage and beliefs. As part of this community we can be confident of expressing our beliefs and practices wherever we go.

VAYERA - *Save the World*

The Talmud teaches that the reason why man was created as a single creation is to teach us that saving one person is equivalent to saving the entire world. It follows, therefore, that every individual has the power to affect the entire world with his actions. Maimonides, in his Laws of *Teshuva*, explains that every person must imagine that the entire world is equally balanced between good and bad deeds and that his personal actions will tip the scales towards life or destruction.

This *Parsha* illustrates this important tenet. When God tells Abraham of the imminent destruction of Sodom, Abraham bargains with Him to spare the city. Abraham begins by asking God to spare the city in the merit of 50 righteous citizens. When God accepts his plea Abraham lowers his offer of righteous citizens by ten until he reaches God's minimum "breaking point" of ten.

If we assume that Sodom and its sister city Amorah had at least five thousand inhabitants, then the good deeds of just .02% would be sufficient to save the entire population. Every two righteous people could save one thousand evil ones.

Our deeds have repercussions far beyond what our minds can logically process. The Kabbalah teaches that everything we do has a corresponding effect in the heavenly spheres. The Talmud relates that each good deed creates an angel that advocates for our benefit, while every sin creates one that prosecutes us.

Each of us has the power to literally save the society we live within with our actions. The very fate of our own great city might, at any moment, be hanging in the balance. The next thing we do right now might tip the scales. Just ten righteous people could have saved the entire populations of Sodom and Amorah. The way we conduct ourselves towards God and towards our fellow man could save our own world.

It really is up to you. You can save the world.

VAYERA – *One with God*

God appears to Abraham at the outset of the *Parsha,* and then Abraham runs off to greet guests. There are many explanations offered by the commentators as to why and how Abraham could "leave" God in the middle of His "visit". I would like to offer another.

When we recite the Shema we are not only proclaiming that God is the only Deity, but that God is the only instance of existence. There is nothing "outside" of God. Therefore, everything is part of God and God is part of everything. That means that every person has a "piece" of God within them. This spark of Divinity is the *Neshama*, the soul.

To allow His creation to exist, God hides His presence. God remains hidden to most people. He appears only to those who seek Him. When a person recognizes that there is Divinity within him he cannot help but be stimulated to perform *mitzvot* as a way of actualizing that holiness within him. This is the meaning of the verse, "*Shiviti Hashem Linegdi Tamid* - I have placed God before me always." It is impossible to sin when one feels that God is a part of him.

It was precisely because God appeared to Abraham that he was able to run off to greet his guests. God appeared to Abraham because he was constantly searching for God. The very realization, or appearance, of God aroused such an incredible outpouring of spirituality and holiness that Abraham could do nothing else but run to do a *Mitzvah*, welcoming the guests. When we realize that we each have a "piece" of the Divine within us we too will steer clear of sin and relentlessly pursue holiness and spirituality.

Reflections

A person who views himself as created in the image of God will be reluctant to sin.

VAYERA - *Taking Responsibility*

In this *Parsha* three angels, disguised as men, visit Abraham and reveal to him God's plan to grant him and Sarah a son. When Sarah hears this she laughs thinking, "how could a woman of ninety possible bear a child?" This laughter, an obvious sign of disbelief in the powers of God, is brought to Abraham's attention by God in the verse, "Why is it that Sarah laughed saying, 'Will I actually bear a child despite my old age?' Is anything beyond God?" When confronted with this Sarah, frightened, denies that she laughed. Abraham immediately replies, "No, you did laugh". This is how the episode ends.

Abraham's response seems gruff and insensitive. Couldn't he give Sarah the benefit of the doubt and assume that she really didn't mean to laugh, or couldn't he just let her mistake "slide" just this once? The *Torah*, through Abraham's reprimand, is teaching us an important lesson. God gave Man the gift of free choice: the power to decide what actions to take in life. With that gift comes responsibility. Man is responsible for the choices he makes.

This is clear in the story of Adam and Eve in the Garden of Eden. When God confronts Adam regarding his sin Adam immediately attempts to absolve himself by blaming Eve. Had Adam taken responsibility for his sin and repented he might not have been banished from Eden. However, since he didn't take responsibility for his actions he could not repent, for the prerequisite for repentance is acknowledgement of wrongdoing. If you didn't sin, what is there to repent for?

Sarah sinned by doubting God's power. She then refused to take responsibility for her actions. Abraham realized that until she did so, she would be unable to repent, receive atonement, and move forward in her path of spiritual growth. Therefore, Abraham forced her to recognize and accept her mistake, thereby allowing her to repent.

In addition, by making sure Sarah took responsibility for her actions Abraham was able to, in some way, repair the damage done by Adam's original shirking of responsibility in Eden.

Finally, the son that is born to Abraham and Sarah as promised is called Yitzchak – meaning, "will laugh". Why would a patriarch of the

Jewish People bear a name derived from a mistake that his mother made by doubting in God's power? The lesson is that once a sin is recognized and repented for it can no longer be counted against a person. In fact, it can be turned into a merit.

Reflections

Admitting that we have done wrong is often the hardest, and most important, part of repentance.

Lot – *Lost and Found*

The character of Lot, Abraham's nephew, plays an important supporting role in the story of Abraham's development into the Patriarch of the Jewish People. When God tells Abraham to leave his homeland for Israel it is a command directed solely to him. The rabbis teach that Lot really was not suppose to be taken on the journey but that he pushed his way in, convincing Abraham to take him along. As a follower of Abraham, Lot learned from his ways but was unable to pass along these teachings to his shepherds and servants. As a result they disregarded all respect for private property and, according to the *Midrash*, allowed Lot's flocks to graze in private lands without permission. Because of this, Abraham separated from Lot.

Separated from Abraham, Lot begins to drift away from Abraham's teachings. His first mistake was his move to Sodom, a city that epitomized evil and cruelty. Despite living in the city, however, Lot continued to practice the primary lesson taught by Abraham: that of hospitality. This is clear from his protection of the messengers who visit his home.

Despite their parting of ways and Lot's drifting from his uncle's teachings, Abraham continues to protect him. The first example of this is during the war of the kings, when Lot is captured and Abraham launches a daring raid to rescue him. The second is when God rescues Lot from the destruction of Sodom in the merit of Abraham and his prayers.

After his rescue from Sodom, Lot is tricked into committing the sin of incest with his daughters, resulting in the birth of two nations: Amon and Moav. Lot is not mentioned again in the *Torah*.

On a symbolic level Lot represents the Jew who is estranged from his heritage but still retains the basic values passed on to him by his ancestors. He lives in a world which disregards the traditions of his past although he tries, against all odds, to hold on to their memory. When it seems as though he will be totally engulfed by society, his heritage lost forever, he is suddenly rescued from annihilation by the power of his divine destiny. There comes a time, however, when he is dragged so deeply into the depths of assimilation and sin that he appears totally and irreversibly lost to his people and heritage.

From the deepest depths of darkness, however, he suddenly and mysteriously is brought back to his home. From the tragic sin of incest that Lot commits is born the nation of Moav, from which is born Ruth, the righteous convert to Judaism and the great grandmother of King David, the Messiah, who will return all the lost Jewish souls to their true home.

The gematria, or numerical value, of Lot is 45, which is equal to the word "Mah" or "what". Lot is the lost Jew, the question waiting to be answered. At the end of the story Lot does return through Ruth. So too, all the lost Jews will be returned to their heritage and destiny by *Mashiach* the son of David, speedily in our days.

CHAYEH SARAH – *Camels*

The *Torah* never wastes words. Every story, description, phrase, and word teaches a unique message or lesson. In the *Parsha*'s account of how Abraham's servant Eliezer finds a mate for Isaac the *Torah* seems to waste words several times in describing the camels that accompanied Eliezer on his journey.

The *Parsha* first tells us that Abraham gave Eliezer ten camels for his journey. Then it describes how the camels were stabled and fed. When Lavan, Rebecca's brother, comes out to greet Eliezer the first thing he notices are the camels. Finally, when Eliezer and Rebecca approach Isaac's home, the first thing Isaac notices are the camels. Why the fascination with camels? What lesson is the *Torah* trying to teach us by describing the role of the camels in such detail?

The Hebrew word for camel is GaMaL. The word GaMaL also means to give or pay. In fact, the term for benefactor is GoMeL *Chesed*. According to tradition Abraham was the physical representation of the Divine attribute of *Chesed*-Giving. Everything that Abraham did was some form of *Chesed*. It was through *Chesed* that Abraham spread the belief in God to the nations. *Chesed* was the banner that Abraham carried, and the flag tied to his flagpole.

When Abraham sent his servant to find a bride for Isaac he specifically sent him to his birthplace for he believed that only there, among his distant relatives, would he find a woman who possessed the quality of *Chesed*. In order to make his intentions clear to everyone, Abraham sent his camels on the journey as representations of *Chesed*. The presence of the camels served as his calling card, identifying his servant as a member of the tribe of *Chesed*. When Lavan went to greet his foreign visitor he saw the camels and immediately knew that Eliezer was on a mission from Abraham. Finally, when Isaac looked up from his prayers and saw the camels approaching, he knew that the woman riding them was a woman of *Chesed*.

Reflections

Every person has a calling card that represents who he is to the world. Abraham's calling card was *Chesed*. We all need to develop our own calling cards to represent us in the most favorable and honorable way possible.

CHAYEH SARAH - *Keep It Simple*

In this *Parsha* our father Abraham sends his servant Eliezer on a mission to find a wife for Isaac. Why didn't Abraham present Eliezer with a long list of criteria for his future daughter in-law? After all, Abraham was the father of the greatest and holiest nation ever to be born, and the wife of his son Isaac would play a major role in its development. The only criterion that Abraham does present is that the woman may not be from the nation of Canaan because the Canaanites did not display the attribute of *Chesed*, the trait of giving, that Abraham embodied. Aside from this condition Abraham left the choice of his future daughter in-law to Eliezer. How could he do that?!

The Rabbis teach that the world was created through *Chesed*. According to the Kabbalah this means that God's only possible reason for creating the world was to "give" solely for the sake of giving. This is the true definition of *Chesed*: to give without expecting anything in return. One of the greatest forms of *Chesed* is love. True love is giving oneself completely to another unconditionally.

Abraham did not have a written *Torah* to follow, yet our Rabbis teach that he kept the entire *Torah*. The essence of the *Torah* is *Chesed* – Giving. Every *Mitzvah* revolves around either giving to another person, giving to God, giving to oneself, or any combination of the three. Abraham, as the embodiment of *Chesed* in the world, was able to fulfill the essence of the entire *Torah* and forge an unmatched relationship with God through *Chesed*.

Abraham understood that the most important trait in a wife for his son is *Chesed* because through *Chesed* a person can reach the highest levels of holiness. If a person embodies true *Chesed* all the other character traits and behaviors fall into the path of holiness with it. Without *Chesed*, nothing else matters regardless of how "holy" it may seem. Therefore, Abraham didn't need to present Eliezer with a checklist for his son's new bride. There was only one requirement: *Chesed*.

Reflections

What are we looking for in a mate? Is Chesed at the top of the list, before wealth, looks, and status? If not, then we should consider rethinking our requirements.

TOLDOS – *Prayer Power*

In this *Parsha* our patriarch Isaac prays for his barren wife Rebecca to conceive, and his prayer is answered. Isaac was forty years old when he married Rebecca and sixty when she conceived. That means that Isaac waited twenty years before praying for his child. Why did Isaac wait twenty long years, while watching his beloved wife suffer tremendous emotional pain, before praying? Couldn't he have prayed after one year, or five, or even ten? The same question can apply to both Abraham and Jacob, who also seemed to wait before praying for their barren wives.

Each of our patriarchs had a relationship with God that was closer than anything possible for any other human being. Their trust and faith in God was absolute. God promised each of them offspring, and they had complete faith that God would fulfill His promise in its proper time. Their relationship and trust were so strong that they possibly felt that asking God for something would, in a way, display a lack of trust.

The matriarchs taught their husbands a very important lesson by urging, almost forcing, them to pray. They taught them that prayer is not a show of distrust and non-belief. Rather, it is a way of strengthening Man's relationship with God, because by praying to God, Man shows that he trusts in His power.

There is another way of answering why the patriarchs waited so long to pray for offspring. True love is unconditional. If a relationship with a friend or spouse is based on what we can get from them, then it is flawed. Because of their uniquely close and intimate relationship with the Almighty the patriarchs could possibly have felt that by asking Him for a "favor" they would be turning their unconditional loving relationship into a conditional and flawed one.

The matriarchs taught them that prayer does not weaken the Man-God relationship. It strengthens it by allowing Man to be vulnerable before God, and by creating the setting for God to give to Man. True love is when both parties can give to and receive from each other unconditionally. Prayer, therefore, is the vehicle for Man to strengthen his relationship with God.

TOLDOS – *The Perfect Blend*

Our forefathers Abraham and Isaac are both given two sons representing the opposite extremes of traits and characteristics. Abraham fathered Isaac and Ishmael, and Isaac fathered Esav and Jacob. It is only Jacob who is finally blessed with twelve sons, all of whom are considered worthy and complete. It is, therefore, only Jacob who is honored with the name Israel, and with having the Jewish people called the Children of Israel.

Why didn't Abraham or Isaac merit this great honor? Why didn't God bless them with perfect sons instead of opposite extremes?

The Kabbalah teaches that Abraham represented the ultimate trait of *Chesed* – Giving and that Isaac represented the ultimate trait of Gevurah – strength or reserve (the ability to hold back). Abraham's name – "father of many nations" – in itself implies *Chesed* while Isaac's name – "laugh" – represents a disbelief in something coming from the outside and a firm belief in what's already within you: *Gevurah*.

Abraham and Isaac represented opposite extremes of character. Extremes can only give birth to other extremes. The Kabbalah teaches that Jacob represents the trait of *Tiferet*, which literally means "beauty", but on a deeper level means "balance". Jacob is called a "tent dweller" by the *Torah*, representing his ability to sit at home and study the holy teachings. At the same time he is described as a powerful man, able to remove the boulder from the well, and a master shepherd, as well as being able to live in a foreign land without losing his own identity. Jacob was able to master both his grandfather's attribute of *Chesed* and his father's attribute of *Gevurah*. Only Jacob's *Tiferet* – Balance could give birth to complete and whole offspring. Only Jacob could bear the title of Israel because the true essence of Israel and the *Torah* of Israel is *Tiferet* - Balance.

Reflections

Judaism is not a religion of extremes. Our Rabbis constantly teach us to take the middle road to attain balance and truth. Every *Mitzvah* in the *Torah*, when studied and analyzed correctly, is rooted in *Tiferet*, whether it's the balance between Man and Man, Man and God, Man and Nature, or Man and Himself.

In order to reach the true middle road, however, we need to internalize and experience the extremes in positive ways. Only when we have studied and experienced the *Chesed* of Abraham and the *Gevurah* of Isaac can we be ready to synthesize the two, and find the beauty and balance of Jacob's *Tiferet*.

TOLDOS – *Jacob's Journey*

As a result of his holding on to the heel of Esau at birth, Isaac named his son Jacob, which is a form of the Hebrew word for heel. Only after eight decades does Jacob receive the name Israel, or Prince of God. Why does the *Torah* refer to the father of the tribes of Israel, and thus, the primary father of the Jewish People, with the seemingly derogatory name meaning "heel" for most of his life?

The *Torah* is teaching us an important lesson. No one starts off as a "Prince of God". It requires years of hard work and growth. Even Jacob, the greatest of the Patriarchs was not born that way. He was born behind the evil Esav, but he did not passively accept his lowly status. Instead, he grabbed onto the heel of Esau and struggled to raise himself up. He continued this struggle for the rest of his life, never resting on his achievements, until he finally merited the name of Israel.

Where we come from is not nearly as significant as where we take ourselves. The *Torah* makes a point of repeating that Rebecca was the daughter of Betuel and the sister of Lavan to emphasize that being raised and taught by evil men did not stop her from becoming a Matriarch and Prophetess. Similarly, Jacob's twenty one years in the house of Lavan did not adversely affect his righteousness.

Although environment is a factor in character growth, our personal striving for excellence is primary. Everyone has the potential to remain a "Heel" or to become the "Prince of God". It is up to each of us to choose our objective and strive with all our power to achieve it. Jacob and Rebecca teach us that we can succeed.

Veyetze - *The Secret Ingredient*

How was Jacob able to maintain his faith and morality in the face of all the negative forces and adversity during his twenty one year exile in Haran? In fact, the Rabbis teach that, all during his difficult exile in Haran, Jacob followed all of the teachings of Abraham and Isaac and stayed completely true to his faith. Of course Jacob had faith in God's promise to protect him and make him into a great nation, but was faith alone enough? Many people have faith, and yet succumb to the pressures and temptations of society — so what was it?

Passion. Jacob had tremendous passion. The dictionary defines passion as "a powerful emotion". You can have faith or you can have passionate faith. You can love or you can passionately love. The same is true of all actions and emotions. Passion turns an ordinary activity into an exciting and stimulating experience.

When Jacob first laid eyes on Rachel, he didn't just politely introduce himself. Instead, he kissed Rachel and cried, because he connected with her so deeply that he could actually see their future together. This was passion. Then Jacob worked for fourteen years to marry her. That's passion! If you think it was lust, just remember that the latter seven years of work were done after he already had married Rachel. The lust was long gone. It was true passion that kept Jacob going strong all those years. Everything he did was with passion, which is the reason that everything he did in Haran was successful. This trait of passion was inherited from his grandfather Abraham who was the embodiment of *Chesed* - Giving, the ultimate extension of which is passion.

Reflections

Be passionate about the things you do. Be passionate about your relationships, instead of just letting them fall into a "regular" pattern. Be passionate about Judaism. Pray with passion. Perform *Mitzvot* with passion.

VAYETZE — *Movement*

The *Parsha* describes movement in different ways. It begins with, "And Jacob departed from Bersheva and went to Haran." The commentaries ask why the *Torah* needed to use both "departed" and "went" instead of just saying "Jacob went to Haran". Rashi cites a *Midrash* that explains that the *Torah* wanted to teach us that when a righteous person leaves a place, that place suffers. In other words, Bersheva suffered a decline when Jacob fled from his brother Esau.

Later in the *Parsha* the *Torah* says, "And Jacob lifted his legs and went to Haran." The commentaries again ask why the need for "lifted his legs" instead of just "went to Haran". Rashi cites a *Midrash* that explains that since this event occurred after God promised to protect Jacob, his heart was so filled with joy that it lifted his legs, making it seem as though they moved on their own.

Reflections

What a difference a positive and optimistic attitude can make? It's so difficult to embark on an unpleasant mission or task. It's even difficult to get up out of bed in the morning when we have nothing good to look forward to in the day ahead. However, when we have something exciting planned for the day we enthusiastically jump out of bed, full of energy.

By viewing our daily tasks in positive ways, we can turn everything we do into enriching and fulfilling experiences. It might not be in our power to choose exactly what we do on a given day, for some things are beyond our control. It is, however, in our control to view everything we do in the way we choose. For example, when we have an unpleasant task to complete at work we can view it as a chance to earn money that we can use for Mitzvot. Attending a funeral or *shiva* house can be viewed as an opportunity to comfort mourners, instead of as a depressing and unpleasant experience.

VAYISHLACH - *Thoughts Count*

After Jacob's daughter Dinah is captured and raped by the prince of Shechem, Jacob's sons, Shimon and Levi, lull the Shechemites into a false sense of security, and then attack and plunder the city and slaughter all the male inhabitants. When Jacob hears of this he scolds his sons for embarrassing him in the eyes of the nations, and for provoking them to attack and destroy him and his people. To this, the brothers respond that they had no choice but to avenge the honor of their sister.

From the continuation of the *Parsha* it seems like the brothers were correct in their revenge. Why then was Jacob so upset at them and afraid of his neighbors? Didn't he have faith in God's protection? Didn't he want to avenge the rape of his beloved daughter?

I think the answer can be found in Jacob's instructions to his sons after the incident. Jacob tells his sons to remove the foreign gods from their midst in order to worship God. Where did these "foreign gods" come from? They came from the booty of Shechem. Jacob agreed that the people of Shechem deserved punishment for their horrible sin, but that the punishment be meted out with pure intentions. By plundering the city and taking its idols, the sons revealed that their intentions were not solely to punish the Shechemites but rather to gain from its plunder.

It was these impure motives, or hypocrisy, that Jacob disapproved of. Jacob's impeccable integrity forced the nations to respect him and his boundaries. Once that aura of integrity and purity was broken by the plunder of Shechem, Jacob feared that the nations would no longer be in awe of him and would try to destroy him. By ordering the destruction of the plunder Jacob restored the integrity of his people in the eyes of the nations and no longer had anything to fear.

VAYISHLACH – *Self*

Upon returning from his twenty one year sojourn in the house of Lavan, Jacob is faced with meeting his brother Esau, who swore to kill him for "stealing" his blessings. Jacob is terrified. He sends messengers to Esau bearing tribute, and splits his camp into two parts, expecting that one might be totally annihilated by Esau. In the midst of these preparations for the feared encounter, Jacob finds himself alone. He is then forced to wrestle with an attacker, who our Sages identify as Esau's guardian angel. As the sun begins to rise and the angel realizes that he cannot prevail, he hits and injures Jacob's thigh, but Jacob refuses to let him go free. When the angel pleads for his freedom Jacob offers it to him in exchange for a blessing, which the angel bestows upon him by changing his name from Jacob, representing a heel, to Israel, representing kingship. When Jacob then asks the angel for his name the angel replies, "Why do you ask for my name?" and blesses him again. This is where the encounter abruptly ends. The angel never does seem to reveal his name to Jacob.

One possible way of understanding Jacob's encounter with the angel is that Jacob was struggling with his own fears and insecurities regarding meeting Esau. He had no confidence in his ability and merit to prevail against his brother and therefore, expected the worst. Before being able to face Esau he first needed to conquer these insecurities and fears. He could only do this alone.

The angel represented his insecurity. Therefore, when Jacob asked the angel for his name the angel did, in fact, answer him. The name of the angel was, "why do you ask for my name", a name that represents the essence of insecurity. I am so insignificant and worthless that, "why would anyone want to know my name?" After defeating the angel, representing his own insecurity, Jacob could finally face Esau.

Most of our own insecurities are rooted in a sense of self deprecation and low self esteem. We must struggle with, and defeat, that angel within us who carries the name of, "why do you ask for my name". Only then can we hope to be blessed with success in our endeavors.

VAYISHLACH – *Starting Up*

When Jacob returns to Israel with his family after twenty one years in the house of Lavan he decides to send messengers to his brother Esau to inform him of his arrival. The medieval commentator Ramban cites a *Midrash* that compares Jacob's action to starting up with a mad dog by grabbing its ears. The Ramban continues the comparison by explaining how the destruction of the second temple began hundreds of years before the event, when the Hasmoneon kings asked the Romans to help resolve a dispute as to who should be king. Once the Romans entered Israel they could not be thrown out. Based on the *Midrash* and commentary, Jacob erred by "waking up" Esau by sending the messengers.

Reflections

The great teachers of Mussar (ethics) extend this idea to include every person's battle against their evil inclination. Many times our evil inclination lies dormant only to be awakened by our own actions. We invite the evil inclination by going places where we know it frequents and by associating with people that are its usual customers. If we just avoided it we could be safe but instead, we send messengers to inform it of our whereabouts and plans.

VAYESHEV – *The Mystery of Life*

The *Parsha* begins by telling us that Jacob settled in the land of his fathers. The *Midrash* comments that Jacob sought to settle down in peace and quiet, but that the incident with his son Joseph ruined his plan. The *Midrash* continues by commenting that the righteous seek to live peaceful lives, to which God remarks, "Isn't it enough that they will enjoy peace in the world to come, but do they want it in this world too?"

This *Midrash* is responding to one of the most difficult theological questions: why do bad things happen to good people? How often do we ask this question in our own lives? We try our hardest to be good people and do the right thing only to discover that, not only were our efforts for naught, but that people who couldn't care less about doing right are rewarded with success. This causes us to question the whole concept of Divine justice, or even worst, the very existence of God.

What is the answer to this question? The *Midrash* doesn't give us one, because there is no answer that we, as human beings, can comprehend. The answer lies in the great and unfathomable mystery of the ways of God. The *Midrash* teaches us that even the greatest and holiest personalities ever to exist faced the same dilemma that we all do. As we read the stories of our holy Patriarchs and Matriarchs we are confronted by tragedy after tragedy. The years of horrible suffering endured by our Matriarchs. The pain of Abraham banishing his first born son and of Isaac witnessing the hatred between his sons. The heartbreak of Jacob upon the death of his beloved Rachel. The sorrow of Jacob who believed that his favorite son Joseph was killed.

Despite all the tragedies and setbacks our Patriarchs and Matriarchs never lost faith in God and they never stopped doing the right thing. They couldn't answer why they deserved such treatment. All they could do is accept that, although the ways of God are unfathomable, His justice is absolute and righteous.

This is one of the greatest lessons that we can learn from the stories of our ancestors. We'll never know why bad things happen to good people, but we can never stop being good people.

Reflections

The mysteries of God are just that: mysteries. We can't expect to find answers for these eternal questions. That doesn't mean that we shouldn't continue to try. It does mean that we should continue our spiritual quest despite not being able to answer or understand everything. Focusing on our inability to find all of the answers will prevent us from growing in the areas that we can understand.

VAYESHEV – *Tzadik*

When we think of a *Tzadik* we imagine a pious looking individual who is almost totally separated from the mundane physical aspects of the world. It is a picture of someone who dresses differently from the norm, avoids contact with those outside of his spiritual realm, and is often oblivious to modern modes and technological advances. The *Torah*, however, paints a very different picture of a *Tzadik*.

Joseph is the only Jewish biblical figure referred to as *Tzadik* by the Sages. A *Tzadik* is someone who never sinned, and Joseph is the one who fit this criterion, for even though he came close to sinning with the wife of his master Potifar, he overcame his evil inclination at the final possible moment and remained pure.

Joseph is described as being very handsome. The *Midrash* comments that he might have even spent a little too much time combing his hair and caring for his appearance. He was so handsome that the wife of Potifar went to great lengths to seduce him. When Jacob blesses his sons on his death bed he refers to Joseph as the handsome one. Clearly, Joseph the *Tzadik* was not only physically attractive but also made the effort to enhance his appearance.

We also learn that Joseph had the ability to make people like him. He first found favor in the eyes of Potifar, then the prison warden, and finally the Pharaoh himself. Joseph also was knowledgeable in the area of economics and diplomacy. He developed and implemented a plan of momentous proportions to feed Egypt during the seven years of famine while simultaneously acquiring all of the farm land for the Pharaoh. He became completely integrated into Egyptian society to the point that even his brothers failed to recognize him as being anyone other than Egyptian royalty.

Despite his appearance, secular knowledge, and total integration into Egyptian society Joseph is still called *Tzadik*. In fact, I believe that it is precisely because of all of these attributes that he was a *Tzadik*. One of the jobs of the *Tzadik*, particularly according to the Chassidic teachings, is to elevate the sparks of holiness found in the mundane and "unholy". Joseph was able to raise up the sparks of holiness in the physical world.

Reflections

Judaism doesn't believe that you have to be celibate or ascetic to be holy. You also don't have to dress in robes and meditate on mountaintops. Anyone can be holy in their normal, physical, and material lives. Holiness is a function of actions and beliefs, not appearances or social status.

VAYESHEV – *Joseph*

After listing the descendents of Esau at the end of the previous *Parsha* the *Torah* begins to recount Jacob's legacy by only mentioning Joseph. The *Midrash* offers several reasons for this focus on Joseph. One is that all the work and hardship that Jacob endured was solely to marry Rachel, Joseph's mother. Another is that Jacob and Joseph shared similar hardships and experiences, such as servitude and fraternal strife.

There is another explanation that reveals the true character and destiny of Joseph. The *Midrash* says that when Jacob saw the long list of Esau's progeny he wondered how they would ever be subdued. In response he was given an analogy of a room packed with flax, with no room left to add more. Then a single spark lights the flax and is able to destroy it all. That spark is Joseph.

Why is Joseph given this unique role as destroyer of Esav? Throughout Rabbinic literature the adjective "*Tzadik*" is appended to Joseph's name. No other biblical figure has this honor of being called "*Tzadik*". The reason for this is that the term *Tzadik* is used to refer to someone who never sinned. According to tradition Joseph fits that description. The most glaring example of this is when Joseph refuses, at the last possible moment, to commit adultery with his master Potifar's wife. He comes close to falling into sin, but he resists and emerges pure and innocent. This is in direct consonance with his brother Judah, who succumbs to his passions and sins with Tamar, but later finds the power to acknowledge his sin and repent. While Joseph is the *Tzadik*, Judah is the Baal Teshuvah, the penitent.

Jewish tradition teaches that there will be two Messiahs in the days of final redemption. The first will be the Son of Joseph who will begin the redemption, but will be killed before completing it. The second will be the Son of David, descendant of Judah, who will succeed in bringing the final and complete redemption of the Jewish People. Why is there a need for these dual Messiahs?

I think the reason is as follows. When facing the nations of the world the Jewish People must do so with absolute purity and integrity, to inspire their awe and respect. Therefore, it must be with the personality of the *Tzadik* that the redemption from the bondage of the nations begins. However, the purity of the *Tzadik* alone cannot accomplish the internal redemption of the Jewish People by lifting them up from the depths of their spiritual bondage. It is only the Baal Teshuvah, the Son of David, who experienced sin and repented, that can redeem the Jews.

This is why Joseph is viewed as the destroyer of Esav, for only with complete integrity and purity will Israel be able to stand up to the nations and ultimately emerge victorious.

MIKEYTZ – *Seeing the Truth*

This *Parsha* recounts the details of Pharaoh's two dreams. In the first, seven fat cows are devoured by seven skinny cows, which remain skinny even after their meal. In the second, seven full sheaves of wheat are devoured by seven threadbare ones, with no change to their threadbare appearance. Pharaoh is bewildered by these dreams and summons the greatest dream interpreters of his kingdom, but none of them can provide him with a sensible interpretation. Only Joseph is able to interpret the meaning of the dreams, predicting seven years of plenty followed by seven years of famine.

According to both Jewish tradition and ancient Egyptian history, the Egyptians were the most highly advanced practitioners of matters of the occult, including dream interpretation. Was there not one wizard from among the greatest wizards of the ancient world who could correctly interpret dreams that appear to be clear in their imagery and message?

I think the Egyptian wizards did understand the imagery of Pharaoh's dreams. However, they were afraid to go out on a limb and interpret the dreams correctly by telling Pharaoh that, instead of enjoying the forthcoming years of plenty, they would have to sacrifice to save food for the years of famine that would follow. What if they were mistaken? The consequences for them would be deadly. In addition, the wizards themselves did not want to accept what they knew was the correct interpretation because it would mean that they too would have to deprive themselves during the years of plenty.

Joseph was the only one brave enough to tell Pharaoh the hard news. He was willing to face the problem and solve it regardless of the consequences. This is the characteristic of a true leader, and this is why Pharaoh chose Joseph to lead Egypt. Not because he was a better wizard, but because he was a brave leader willing to take a stand for what he believed to be true.

There is another reason why only Joseph was willing to correctly interpret Pharaoh's dreams. When Pharaoh asked him for his interpretation, Joseph responded that it was God who placed the interpretation into his mouth. Joseph realized that Man has no control over his destiny. Therefore, he could speak the truth freely, knowing that only God would determine his future. The Egyptians had no faith in a God Who controls Man's destiny and, therefore, refrained from telling Pharaoh the truth, because they feared the consequences of their words.

VAYIGASH – *Is My Father Still Alive?*

Immediately after revealing his identity to his brothers Joseph asks them, "Is my father still alive?" The brothers are too shocked and terrified to respond. Joseph then calls them closer and tells them that he is their brother and that they should not fear the consequences of their actions against him.

Throughout the meeting and confrontation between Joseph and his brothers the brothers constantly refer to their father Jacob. Why then does Joseph ask them if Jacob is still alive? Isn't it obvious from the story of his brothers that he is? Furthermore, why don't the brothers answer Joseph's question in the affirmative? In fact, Joseph's question is never answered and Joseph doesn't repeat the question to force an answer. What then is the true meaning and purpose of the original question?

According to the *Midrash* Joseph's question is not really a question but rather a rebuke. How? According to the Talmud Jacob represented the attribute of truth. He also represented holiness, spirituality, and faith in God. Joseph couldn't understand how the brothers could have committed such a terrible act against him in the face of, and under the spiritual influence of, Jacob. "Is my father still alive" was not really a question. It was a rebuke to be read as "is the truth, justice, and piety that my father represented no longer in existence that you felt empowered to commit a despicable sin against me? Is truth and justice (Jacob) still alive in the world?"

When the brothers heard this rebuke they were terrified. There was no acceptable answer. The *Midrash* on this tells us to imagine how much more terrifying will the rebuke of God be when we reach the next world after our hundred and twenty years of life.

The true answer to Joseph's question or rebuke lies within each of us. We have the ability to make sure that truth and justice are always protected and upheld so that when that day finally comes when we stand before the Master of the World, after hundred and twenty years, we will not tremble in fear but instead confidently answer the question with a resounding, "yes. Our father Jacob is alive and well."

VAYIGASH – *Who Will Save Us?*

The *Parsha* of Vayigash opens with a confrontation between brothers Yehudah and Joseph that leads to the final reconciliation between Joseph and his brothers. According to our mystical sources this confrontation represents an ongoing struggle between the different attributes and forces each one represents.

Joseph is the only biblical personality referred to by our Sages as a *Tzadik*, a righteous person who has never succumbed to his desires and acted upon them. In all his years in the hedonistic society of Egypt, whether as slave or ruler, Joseph never allowed his "evil inclination" to get the better of him. This aspect of purity was inherited from his mother Rachel who, the *Torah* tells us, was beautiful, innocent, and pure.

Yehudah is the son of Leah, the sister who was not so beautiful, whose eyes were weak from tears and who had to resort to trickery to marry Jacob. The *Torah* deviates from its major story line to tell us of Yehudah's romantic encounter with a woman who he thinks is a prostitute but who in fact is his daughter in-law Tamar.

Yehudah seems quite far from being a *Tzadik* and yet, he inherits the blessing of kingship and becomes the ancestor of King David and the Messiah while Joseph, the *Tzadik*, and his descendents move to the sidelines of Jewish history. There is even a rabbinic tradition that there will be two Messiahs. The first will be the "Son of Joseph" who will be killed, to be followed by the "Son of David" who will usher in the Messianic era. Why isn't Joseph chosen to be the progenitor of the Messiah, and what did Yehudah do to deserve the honor?

After Yehudah lives with Tamar she becomes pregnant with his child and is taken in front of the court to be stoned for adultery. When Tamar presents to the court the staff and seal that Yehudah gave her as payment, Yehudah publicly admits his sin with the words "*Tzadka Mimeni* – she is more righteous than I". Yehudah becomes the model of the Baal Teshuvah by recognizing his failure, admitting it, and changing his ways to become better. A thousand years later King David does the same thing after sinning with Batsheva.

The Jewish people are not perfect. They stumble and sin, but then they pick themselves up and try to be better. Therefore their salvation, the Messiah, can't be someone who has never sinned, for how will he know how to deal with a people that stumble? Only a Messiah who is a "Baal Teshuvah" can save Israel. Only a Messiah who comes from Leah, the unloved wife, Yehudah, Ruth the convert, and King David the penitent can save the Jewish nation. Joseph, the *Tzadik*, is needed to pave the way by serving as a model to motivate the Jews into recognizing who they are and what they need to do but, only Yehudah, the Baal Teshuva, can bring them back from the depths to the heights of redemption and salvation. May we merit seeing that redemption very soon.

VAYECHI – *The Stage is Set*

In this *Parsha* of *Vayechi* Jacob blesses his sons, as well as Joseph's two sons, before his passing at the age of one hundred and forty seven. The *Parsha*, and the book of Genesis, end with the passing of Joseph at the age of one hundred and ten.

It is difficult to define the character and ultimate role of Joseph in the *Torah*, for as great as the Bible and the Rabbis make him out to be, he still ends up taking second place to Judah, who receives the blessing of kingship and leadership from Jacob and ultimately becomes the forbearer of the Messiah. Not even one of the twelve tribes of Israel is named after Joseph although his sons Menashe and Ephraim each get their own tribe. In fact, Joseph's name seems to disappear from the focus of Jewish history after his death.

Many years ago I had the honor of hearing the Rosh Yeshiva of the famous Lakewood Yeshiva, Rabbi Shnuer Kotler Z"L (may his memory be a blessing for us), speak to a few students privately about Joseph. My understanding of what he said was that Joseph represents Divine Providence, since anyone following his story can only explain the chain of events that led him from a pit in Canaan to the throne in Egypt as Divine Providence.

At the end of the *Parsha*, when the brothers plead with Joseph not to take vengeance upon them after the death of Jacob, Joseph reassures them by saying that regardless of their harmful intentions against him, God manipulated the events to make them culminate for the good of the Jewish nation. Joseph was able to see the hand of God where no one else could. Perhaps this was because he was a dreamer with the ability to look beyond the practical and see the subtle workings of the Divine behind the scenes.

Joseph taught his brothers how to recognize Divine Providence and thus prepared the way for them to survive the exile of Egypt. His perfection (he is the only Biblical figure called a *Tzadik* by the Rabbis) and his sensitivity to the spiritual subtleties that made him a dreamer were not, however, the qualities needed to lead the Jewish people in the exile and in the land of Israel. Only a powerful and practical figure like Judah, the lion, could fulfill that role.

There is a rabbinic tradition that there will be two Messiahs. The first will be the "Son of Joseph" and he will be killed in his mission. The second will be the "Son of David" (Judah) and he will be the savior of Israel. In the book of Genesis Joseph sets the stage for the final salvation of the Jewish people by teaching them how to live in exile while holding firm to their belief in the Divine Providence of God. It is Judah, the powerful lion, who will bring about the final and eternal redemption, speedily in our days.

Reflections

It's not always easy to see the hand of God in the world. We usually only recognize it after the fact. For example, a person might be furious for missing his flight. It is only after he hears the news of the plane crashing that he recognizes Divine Providence in his life. Our challenge is to see God's hand in everything that happens as it is happening.

VAYECHI – *Comforts*

The completion of the book of Genesis marks the beginning of the Jewish exile in Egypt. Exile is commonly understood as being the forceful expulsion of a person or group of people from their homeland. The two post-Egypt exiles of the Jewish People were precipitated first by the Babylonians and then by the Romans. Each exile resulted in the destruction of the Temple in Jerusalem, the destruction of the Land of Israel, the slaughter of hundreds of thousands of Jews and the expulsion of the survivors from the land. These two exiles are mourned and commemorated even to this day.

The beginning of the Egyptian exile was different than the other two in that it did not begin with destruction and tragedy. The Jews came down to Egypt to find one of their own as prime minister, a plentiful food supply in a time of famine, and the finest real estate graciously handed to them. Their situation drastically improved by going into "exile". Also, while the other exiles were caused by Israel's sins the Egyptian exile seems to have no evident cause. In fact, God even told Jacob to bring his family there.

Although we know that it was necessary, as part of God's plan, for the Jews to suffer through the Egyptian exile, there still must be a cause to effect that punishment. What was the sin of Jacob and his family, the Jewish People, which caused the exile?

The Jews came to Egypt during the seven years of famine and Joseph not only provided for their sustenance but also gave them the best land to settle and the means to financially prosper. The *Torah* tells us that they did, in fact, greatly prosper and multiply in number.

When the seven years of famine ended and the situation returned to normal the Jews should have returned to Israel, their home. Why didn't they?

The answer is a familiar one to most of us. The Jews became comfortable in their prosperity. They had the finest homes in the finest neighborhoods, their economic ventures were flourishing and their own brother was second to Pharaoh. Things couldn't have been better, so why leave?

The Jews forgot how they and their fathers had heard the word of God and experienced the Divine Presence in the Land of Israel. They traded spiritual growth and fulfillment in Israel for material comfort in Egypt.

Reflections

There is nothing intrinsically sinful about material comfort. In fact, it is something that we are encouraged to strive for. The sin is when we let that comfort completely engulf us to the extent that we forget our spiritual goals and aspirations. It's so easy to fall into a comfortable groove and forget about the important things in life. Our challenge is to enjoy our comforts while still fully pursuing our spiritual goals, even if it might sometimes be a little uncomfortable.

The Book
of
Shmot

"Exodus"

Sнмот - *From the Depths*

In the *Parsha* of *Shmot* we are introduced to Moses, the future savior, or Messiah, of the Jewish People. Instead of having the glorious and auspicious youth and young adulthood befitting a Jewish Messiah, Moses is delivered into the hands of the Pharaoh and raised in his palace. What a place to train the Jewish Messiah? In the greatest den iniquity known to the ancient world! Does that make sense?

If we look back carefully upon the events of the book of Genesis we see a pattern regarding the saviors of the Jewish People.

Jacob, the actual father of the tribes of "Israel", is compelled to spend twenty one years of his productive adult life in the house of Laban, considered by tradition to be one of the greatest evildoers and enemy of the Jews. The Rabbis even feel the special need to inform us that Jacob kept true to his heritage during this oppressive period of time.

Joseph too is forced to spend nearly twenty years away from his family in the foreign surroundings of Egypt, while resisting the temptations of sex and power. Even Judah, the progenitor of the final and ultimate Messiah, goes through an episode with his daughter in-law Tamar that throws him into the depths of immorality before he prevails over his inclinations and rises to the highest levels of repentance and purity.

The pattern is clear. The saviors of Israel need to endure a period of hardship and tribulation before being able to carry out their mission. The same is true of the Jewish People as a whole. In order to merit acquiring the land of Israel, the Jews had to endure a period of bitter exile in Egypt. The exile acted as a means of purification to allow them to reach levels of spirituality that would otherwise have been unattainable.

Moses needed to experience his own metaphysical exile as a prerequisite to becoming the savior. Like the saviors before him he needed to face challenges to show that he could overcome them. He needed to recognize the trials and conflicts that Jews struggle with to be able to save them from those very things.

Reflections

Jewish saviors are not born as such. They must earn their destiny by hard work and sacrifice.

True greatness implies growth, not perfection. True salvation comes only through growth. The Sages of the *Mishnah* teach that the measure of fulfillment a person feels is based on the amount of effort he invests in the process. It takes hard work, and sometimes even pain, to grow, but the results are noticeable and appreciated.

SHMOT – *What's in a Name?*

The book of *Shmot*, or Names, begins with a roll call of the names of the Jewish People that went down to Egypt. The Rabbis teach that when they were finally taken out of Egypt one of the things that distinguished the Jews from the Egyptians was that they didn't change their Jewish names. What is so important about a name, to merit redemption?

In the first book of Genesis God brings all the animals of the world before Adam and Adam gives each one a name. What this means is that Adam classified each animal and named it based on its character and uniqueness. The name given was not random. It defined the essence of the animal.

The names kept throughout the Egyptian bondage defined the essence, or soul, of every individual Jew which could never be touched by the Egyptians. Those souls remained pure and therefore, merited redemption.

Reflections

Every person has a soul that is pure. Although we can block it with our sins and apathy, we can never soil its essence. The soul awaits the moment when it can finally exercise its spiritual power. All we need to do is let it happen by not stopping it. Most of us are too afraid to let that happen, so we just continue to ignore and suppress our souls. Getting in touch with our essence means tapping into the immense spiritual energy that is within us by allowing it to affect us.

SHMOT – *Never Too Big*

After God tells Moses to go to Egypt to redeem the Jewish people, Moses immediately sets off on the journey with his wife Tzippora and son Gershom. On the way they stop at an inn, where Moses encounters God, and God attempts to kill him. Seeing this, Tzippora takes a stone and circumcises Gershom, abating God's wrath and saving Moses. Why does God want to kill Moses after commanding him to save the Jewish People?

Perhaps Moses thought that since he was on a mission of such enormous importance he did not have to concern himself with the comparatively "mundane" day to day commandments? Isn't the salvation of the Jewish nation more important than the circumcision of a single child? God's response to Moses was blatantly clear. Even the Messiah has to adhere to all of the commandments.

Reflections

It's important to see the big picture, but not at the expense of the details. There are situations where the greater good must take precedents over the fate of individuals. Governments often make decisions based on this. However, there are very few individuals who have the level of importance that warrants hurting others to gain their objectives. Those who actually are "that important" agonize over their decisions and would rather sacrifice themselves than hurting another.

We should never think that our objectives our worthy enough to allow us to overlook the affect our actions have on others. It's not all about the big picture.

VAERA – *Plagues*

The first few portions of the book of *Shmot* describe the ten plagues unleashed by God against Egypt. After each plague Pharaoh is given the opportunity to release the Jews from bondage and bring an end to the plagues, but each time he refuses. Why did God choose to go through this drawn out process of incrementally punishing Egypt instead of simply freeing the Jews in one great miraculous act?

One answer is that on a mystical level each plague was in direct retribution for a particular sin perpetrated by the Egyptians. For example, since the Egyptians threw Jewish children into the rivers several of the plagues, such as blood and frogs, were orchestrated through those same rivers.

There is, I think, another answer which teaches us a great lesson. When God charges Moses with the mission of telling Pharaoh to free the Jews He tells him that He will show the Egyptians, in no uncertain terms, that He is God. Clearly then, the main purpose of the plagues was to make the Egyptians accept God's supremacy. Had they recognized this after the first plague, the next nine would not have been necessary. Instead, however, Pharaoh denied God's supremacy after each plague, and God continued reminding Egypt that He is the Master of the World.

Reflections

God occasionally sends the world reminders that there is a Creator running the world and that we, the citizens of that world, need to lead our lives with that awareness. Unfortunately, many of those reminders come in the form of tragedies and misfortunes. It is not our place to judge why bad things happen to people. It is our obligation, however, to

react to those unfortunate events by making our own lives more meaningful and becoming better people.

Right after the horrendous tragedy of 9-11 almost every New Yorker, and possibly every American, took a long hard look at his life with the new realization that it could be over at any moment without warning. People felt an overwhelming need to find meaning in their lives. Many made drastic changes. Some left lucrative, but unfulfilling, corporate careers to follow what they felt to be their true calling. Some changed the nature of their personal relationships, precipitating a deluge of engagements and marriages. Everyone in New York City suddenly become a bit nicer and more patient and caring towards their fellow citizen. We all took the tragedy as a wake up call from God to refocus our lives from the trivial and empty, to the meaningful and fulfilling.

Now, a few years later, things seem to have come back to the way they were before the tragedy. That is human nature. When times are good, we tend to forget about the important things in life in our preoccupation with the pursuit of success and prosperity. We forget about God and the true purpose of our existence. By so doing, we force God to remind us every so often to put our lives back on track.

Fortunately, God's reminders do not only come in the form of tragedy. Every week God sends us a reminder, the *Shabbat*. On *Shabbat* we recognize that God is the Creator, by refraining from performing creative acts ourselves. We refocus our lives from the material to the spiritual. We exchange the pursuit of financial success for the pursuit of spiritual peace and closeness to God and to our families and friends. On *Shabbat* we experience the ideal of what our lives could and should be.

We should take the beautiful reminder of the *Shabbat* as an opportunity to reevaluate our lives every week and to make the necessary adjustments to put ourselves back on the true path of meaning and fulfillment.

VAERAH – *True Power*

This *Parsha* recounts the first seven plagues that God set upon the Egyptians. The Egyptians were able to survive the first plague of Blood without it being retracted. In fact, the Egyptian sorcerers were able to duplicate the Blood. They were also able to duplicate the second plague, Frogs, but Pharaoh was forced to beg Moses to retract the plague in exchange for letting the Jews leave to worship in the desert. Moses then prayed to God to remove the frogs from Egypt, only to discover that Pharaoh was not planning to keep his end of the deal. This pattern, of Pharaoh breaking his promises to Moses after each plague is removed, continues until the final plague.

Why didn't Moses just let the plague continue until the Jews were actually out of Egypt before praying for it to stop? Didn't Moses realize that Pharaoh was lying to him? Also, wouldn't it make more sense for the Egyptian sorcerers to stop the plagues of Blood and Frogs instead of duplicating them?

There are a few reasons given for why God didn't just let one plague force Pharaoh to release the Jews. One reason is that each plague had a specific part to play in the rehabilitation, or Tikkun, of the Egyptians. Another reason is that God wanted the world to see the power of his judgment.

I think that the reason Moses kept on falling for Pharaoh's lies was because it was God's desire to redeem the Jewish People from Egypt through "*Chesed* – Giving-Kindness" as opposed to harsh judgment. This attribute of *Chesed* is what separated the Jews from the Egyptians. It defined the character of the Jewish People. In order to leave their exile and embark upon their journey to spiritual and physical freedom their redemption had to be orchestrated with *Chesed*. Therefore Moses kept on having mercy on Pharaoh and praying for the plagues to stop.

This also explains why the Egyptian sorcerers were only able to imitate the initial plagues and not stop them. The forces of darkness harnessed by the sorcerers could only produce destruction. Only the power of *Chesed* can stop destruction and produce peace. May we all merit to be redeemed, on a personal and national level, through *Chesed*.

Bo – *The Big Difference*

The *Torah* and the Sages teach that the Jews were spared the hardships of the plagues. For example, while the Egyptian was stricken with boils the Jew standing beside him was completely healthy. The final plague, however, presented a different scenario. God tells Moses to tell the Jews to place the blood of the slaughtered paschal lamb on the doorposts of their homes as a sign for Him to pass over them when smiting the first born of Egypt. It follows that those Jews who chose not to place this sign upon their doors were smitten along with the Egyptians. Why was this final plague different than the first nine where the Jews were spared from the fate of the Egyptians? Why was blood chosen to be the sign that would save the Jews from the fate of the Egyptians?

The *Torah* teaches that God unleashed his complete destructive power (*Mash-cheet*) against the Egyptians in the final plague. This terminology is not used regarding the other plagues possibly because the other plagues were intended not to kill the Egyptians, but to make them accept God's supremacy. The Jews already accepted and believed in God so they didn't need to experience the plagues. The final plague was no longer to teach. Rather it was to destroy and punish. When God's attribute of strict judgment is unleashed it makes no exceptions. All are judged equally. There is no mercy.

The Sages teach that the Jews were on the forty ninth level of impurity in Egypt, with fifty being the absolute lowest. If they had reached fifty they would not have been redeemed. At the splitting of the sea the angels asked God why he would choose to save the Jews and kill the Egyptians, since both nations worshipped idols and were not much different. Therefore, it is clear that were they to be judged with the attribute of strict judgment the Jews might very well be liable to suffer the same punishment as the Egyptians.

Why was blood chosen as the sign to save them? The Sages teach that the original cause of the Egyptian bondage was the "*lashon hara*" or "evil speech" that Joseph spoke against his brothers, which began the chain of events that brought the Jews to Egypt. They also teach that the Jews were redeemed from Egypt because they did not speak *Lashon Hara*. The *Midrash* says that the Jews didn't change their language to that of the Egyptians meaning, I think, that they didn't speak *Lashon Hara*.

The Hebrew word for blood is "*Daam*" which is also the root of the Hebrew word for "silence". Therefore, the blood that the Jews placed on their doorposts represented their merit that differentiated them from the Egyptians: they didn't speak *Lashon Hara*.

Reflections

A religious person is usually thought of as being one who observes rituals. Although this is true, the main characteristic of a religious person is how he interacts with people. Speech is our main form of interaction with society. That's why we must always be careful regarding the words that leave our mouths. Words can destroy. They can also create.

Bo- *Darkness*

When you apply pressure to compel someone to do something you gradually increase the pressure level until they finally succumb. This seems to have been the general structure of the ten plagues. Each plague was progressively more severe until the final one, the killing of the first born, succeeded in forcing Pharaoh's hand. The only problem with this theory is the ninth plague of Darkness. According to our theory it would follow that, based on its position right before the final plague, Darkness was the second most severe plague. The Rabbis explain that the plague of Darkness was so thick that the Egyptians were actually prevented from moving. Each Egyptian was isolated for the three days of the plague. Is this really more severe than being attacked by wild animals, or being stricken with terrible skin diseases, or being bombarded by fire and brimstone? Why then was Darkness used as the ninth, or second to last, plague?

There are two approaches that can be taken to answer this question. The first approach is that the plague of Darkness was actually worse than all the other plagues preceding it because it represented not only a physical condition but also a mental and spiritual condition. One of the symptoms of depression is the inability to move. A depressed person can't even get out of bed. On a deeper level a depressed person feels that there is no reason to move because their situation is utterly hopeless. Depression is, in a way, hopelessness. When a person loses hope and stops trying to move to a better reality he falls into a mental and spiritual coma. This is what the Egyptians were stricken with at the plague of Darkness. In fact, the *Torah* never says that Moses prayed for the plague of Darkness to cease. Therefore, it's quite possible that the depression that engulfed the Egyptians continued through the Exodus.

The second approach is that the plague of Darkness was, in fact, not as severe as the preceding plagues. God, however, wanted to give the Egyptians the opportunity to really think about their situation, to allow them to make the right decision for their future. When individuals become part of a greater unit they often get carried away by the "team spirit". Loyalty to a team is what makes people fans of teams that perennially lose. Although "Team Egypt" was taking a beating with plague after plague, the Egyptian "fans" stayed loyal to their team and actually got more stubborn in their loyalty and "team spirit". Therefore, God broke up the team with Darkness to give every individual Egyptian the chance to be alone. This way they could think of their situation without the enthusiasm and energy of being part of a team.

Reflections

Being alone can have both positive and negative results. Although it's important to take time alone to really think about our lives, goals, and relationships it is also vital to be part of a community that promotes and encourages growth and achievement.

Bo – *Creation and Redemption*

There are two events that we remember and commemorate regularly: the creation of the world and the Exodus from Egypt. Although the creation of the world is a much grander event deserving of humanities recognition, we only remember it in our weekly *Shabbat* prayers. The Exodus from Egypt, however, is mentioned in our morning and evening prayers every day. Why the difference?

The Hebrew word for world, "*Olam*", comes from the word meaning "hidden". The name of God used in Creation, "*Elo-him*", is the numerical equivalent of "Nature". God is hidden in Nature, His creation. The workings of nature are miraculous. However, God created the world in a way to make it seem that nature operates automatically, even though the world could not exist for even a moment without the "will" of the Creator sustaining it.

The Exodus from Egypt represented the revelation of God to the world. Until then only select individuals, such as the Patriarchs and Matriarchs, had an awareness of God's involvement in the world. The rest of the world, represented by Pharaoh, lacked that awareness. They denied in the Creator and His active role in the world. Therefore, God sent Moses to help Pharaoh gain this awareness. If Pharaoh could see the hand of God in nature, then the exile would immediately end, because exile is, essentially, distance from God. This distance can only occur when God is "hidden" from us, which really means, when we are unaware of Him. When there is true awareness of God, there cannot be "exile – distance".

The first nine plagues were all rooted within the laws of nature, albeit extreme aberrations of those laws. The challenge was for Pharaoh to recognize the Hand of God in nature through these plagues. When he was unable to see God in nature, God showed him, and the world, His power in a supernatural way – the killing of every first-born in Egypt. This is why God places so much emphasis on the fact that He, Himself, smote the Egyptians and redeemed the Jewish People. For the first time in history God was no longer "hidden" within nature.

The Exodus represented the revelation of God's presence in the world. With that revelation the exile immediately ended and the Jews were released from bondage. The Talmud teaches that the redemption occurred as quickly as "the blink of an eye". This could refer to "awareness", which occurs in an instance. In the instant that the world gained awareness of God, the exile was over. We remember this "awareness" twice every day. Faith is the constant awareness of God in the world.

Reflections

The Hebrew word for Egypt, *Mitzrayim*, comes from the root word meaning "narrow". In the mystical writings, broadness of mind is characterized by an awareness of God's ever present role in the world and the attempt to attain greater spirituality and closeness to God. Narrowness of mind is the opposite. *Mitzrayim* represents Man's focus on the material world and the laws of nature. In *Mitzrayim* God is hidden from Man, and Man attempts to hide from God. *Mitzrayim* creates great distance between Man and God.

What exactly is exile? Exile is distance from God. How can Man become distant from an ever present God? It occurs when God is hidden from Man. God is hidden in the exile. This is referred to as "*Hester Panim*".

The redemption from Egypt is behind the reason why we connect the blessing of redemption to the *Amidah*. Before engaging in direct dialogue with God we first need to redeem ourselves from the narrowness of mind of *Mitzrayim*. The redemption from *Mitzrayim* represents Man's ongoing struggle to draw close to God.

BISHALACH – *Satisfaction*

This *Parsha* describes the miracle of the Manna, the mysterious food delivered daily by God to the Jews in the wilderness. The *Torah* says that the Manna looked like white coriander seed and tasted like some sort of dough fried in honey.

One of the most popularized Midrashic passages explains that the Manna actually tasted like anything the eater desired, from french fries to pizza to ice cream. Taken literally, as all children and most adults do, this *Midrash* blatantly contradicts the *Torah*'s clear and straightforward description. There must then be a deeper way of understanding this *Midrash*.

There is one verse in the *Ashrei* prayer, which we recite three times daily, that is of such significance that it must be repeated if not said with the proper level of concentration. The verse states, "*Poteach et yadecha, umasbiah likol chai ratzon* – You open your hand, and satisfy the desire (*Ratzon*) of all living beings." This is the common translation. If taken literally, however, the verse means, "You open your hand, and satisfy all living beings with *Ratzon*." *Ratzon* literally means "will", as in, the will to survive. When a person desires something with all his "will" it becomes valuable in his eyes even though that same thing might be worthless to someone else. The Mishnah teaches that a rich person is one who is satisfied with his lot. Therefore a person with very little can feel rich, while a person with much material wealth can feel poor. We therefore ask God to satisfy us by giving us the *Ratzon*, or will, to be happy with what we have.

When the *Midrash* teaches that the Manna could taste like anything the eater wished for, it is reinforcing this lesson of *Ratzon*. Those who had true faith in God and were thankful for His gifts were as happy with the Manna as with their most desired food. Their *Ratzon* could turn a piece of dough into a sumptuous meal.

Reflections

The Manna teaches us an important lesson. It's not what, or how much, we have but rather how we view it and appreciate it. If it is valuable in our own eyes then it will satisfy us and make us happy.

Material wealth does not guarantee happiness. There are incredibly wealthy people who are depressed and unhappy with their lives, and there are paupers who are happy.

We should all be blessed with the Ratzon to appreciate the gifts that we all possess and thereby find true satisfaction in our lives.

BISHALACH - *To Scream or Be Silent*

In this *Parsha* the Jewish People find themselves standing at the shores of the Sea of Reeds with the Egyptians rapidly approaching in pursuit. The Jews cry out in terror and despair to Moses, who admonishes them to "be silent for God will fight for you". Moses then cries out to God who responds, "Why are you screaming to me? Tell the Jews to travel forward".

In both of these dialogues the "screamer" is told to remain silent. Aren't we supposed to scream and cry to God when we need help? Isn't that what prayer is all about? Judaism teaches us not to rely on miracles but rather to do our utmost to make something turn out the way we want it to. Why then did Moses tell the Jews to remain silent and to rely on God to fight their battles?

In 1991, I was studying at the Gruss Kollel in Jerusalem when the first Gulf War broke out. The air raid sirens would sound on a regular basis as Sadaam launched his scud missiles against Israel. As much as the Israeli people desired to use their air force to strike back they couldn't because George Bush, the US president, demanded that they hold back in order to insure the unity of the "coalition" that included several Arab countries. The people of Israel could not fight back. They had no other choice but to run to their shelters, pray, and wait out the storm. This was a time when the Jews had to remain silent and let God fight for them and this is, in fact, what transpired.

There are times when we must keep silent and rely solely on the protection of God. In general, however, the response that God gives to Moses should be our guide. While God does tell Moses and the Jews to stop screaming and to remain silent, He more importantly tells the Jews to "travel forward". Although prayer is important, there is a time for prayer and then there is a time for action. At a certain point prayer must be superseded by action. As Jews we need to scream and cry to God, but then we need to move forward and make things happen. Moving forward is the greatest sign of "*bitachon*", trust in God, because when we attempt to actualize our plans we are trusting that God will help us succeed. When we hold ourselves back we are revealing our doubt, fear, and lack of faith.

Let's all show our faith and trust in God by taking action to realize our goals and dreams to make our community and world a better place.

BISHALACH – *Journey to Teshuvah*

The *Parsha* begins by saying that God decided not to lead the Jews to Israel via the coastal highway, towards the territory of the Philistines, because "it was close" and when they would encounter war they would try to return to Egypt. The literal structure of the verse declares that one of the reasons for not leading the Jews towards the land of the Philistines was because it was close. Why would proximity be a reason not to lead the Jews there?

Instead, God leads the Jews into the wilderness away from Egypt but then tells them to turn back towards Egypt and to camp in front of Baal Tzephon with their backs to the Sea of Reeds. Baal Tzephon was a Mesopotamian deity and, according to Rashi, the last and only Egyptian God remaining in tact after the plagues. Why did God tell the Jews to turn back to Egypt and to camp in front of an idolatrous deity?

The redemption of the Jews from Egypt was not only a physical exodus from bondage. It was also a spiritual breakout from the "narrowness" or unawareness of God, represented by Egypt. While describing the physical exodus the *Torah* is also guiding the repentant along the proper path to personal redemption.

When a person initially breaks from his past behavior he often needs to stay completely away from those things "close" to his past that might remind him of that past and compel him to return to his old ways. This is represented by the way of the Philistines that was "close". Instead, he must journey into the wilderness, which represents isolation or solitude, in order to allow himself the opportunity to reflect upon, and gain strength in, his new path.

The Jews needed to confront the idolatry of Baal Tzephon and the Egyptians in order to move forward in their path to redemption. Moses tells the Jews to take one last look at the Egyptians, "for as you have seen Egypt today, you shall not see them ever again." The allure of Egypt and what it represented would be gone forever. Only after this final confrontation was total redemption possible.

Reflections

There often comes a time in a person's journey towards repentance when he his forced to confront his past. When I was in the process of becoming totally observant, at age fourteen, and I was struggling with observing *Shabbat* at home without a community to join with, I was invited to join my family for an outing at the beach on Saturday. My whole extended family would be there and the weather was beautiful. My alternative would be to spend that *Shabbat* day home alone. As I was just at the beginning of my *Shabbat* observance I was not strong enough to resist the pull of a fun day at the beach with my family, so I went. I don't remember anything specific that happened that day. All I remember is that I felt miserable, and that I vowed never again to violate my *Shabbat* observance. I never have. What looked so normal and enticing in the past had become abnormal and repulsive. Experiencing those feelings was a necessary step in my journey to personal redemption.

YITRO – *On Eagles' Wings*

Before giving them the *Torah* God tells the Jews that if they listen to Him and follow His covenant they will be a chosen people to Him. God begins this message with the verse, "You saw what I did to Egypt and how I carried you on Eagles' Wings and brought you to Me." What is the significance of the comparison to "eagles' wings"?

Rashi, the classic biblical commentator, explains that all other birds carry their young beneath them when in flight to protect them from attacks by other birds. Since the eagle fears no other bird, but only fears man, it carries its young on top of its wings to protect it from arrows. The eagle would rather have the arrow injure it than its offspring.

This analogy between God and eagles is poignant but not totally accurate. Is it possible for God to be injured by man? What then is God's sacrifice in protecting the Jewish People?

Although all physical qualities are obviously irrelevant when relating to God it is possible for God's Name or reputation to be desecrated. In fact, the third of the Ten Commandments prohibits exactly that: using God's Name in vain. One of the gravest sins is *Chillul Hashem*, desecrating God's holy name.

When the world mocks, denigrates, and attacks the Jewish People they are also doing the same to her eagle and protector. By choosing the Jewish People as His holy nation and attaching His Name to them God, so to speak, exposes Himself to desecration. This can only be out of true and everlasting love. It is the unique relationship that exists between the Master of the World and His chosen people.

YITRO – *Leadership*

Leaders usually pass on their positions to their heirs. Why then didn't Moses pass on his position as leader of the Jewish nation to his sons instead of to his student Joshua? They must have learned the secrets of the *Torah* from their father, and possessed many of his qualities and characteristics. Wouldn't that suffice to make them the best choice for taking his place?

According to the timeline of the *Torah* the son's of Moses joined the Jews either right before or right after the giving of the *Torah* at Mount Sinai (there are two opinions in the commentaries). They missed the Egyptian bondage, the Exodus, the splitting of the sea, and possibly the revelation at Mount Sinai.

A Jewish leader must share in the experiences of the Jewish People. He must experience their hardships and sorrows as well as their joys and victories. Moses' sons lacked that experience.

YITRO – *A New Idea?*

In this *Parsha* Moses' father-in-law Yitro observes that Moses is not capable of consistently judging all of the Jewish People alone and therefore suggests that he create a judicial system for the nation, and personally adjudicate only the most difficult and important cases. Yitro's suggestion is presented by Moses to God, and it is accepted and implemented.

Didn't Moses realize that he would be unable to single handedly act as judge for an entire nation? Did he really need Yitro to point this fact out to him?

I once heard a Chassidic explanation that taught the following. Moses was on such a high spiritual level that his countenance actually radiated holiness and purity. When Jews would come before him with a disagreement and see his holy face they would be overwhelmed by holiness and immediately drop their quarrel and make peace. He also realized that teaching by example is so much more effective than teaching by instruction.

Anyone who has had the merit of a face to face encounter with a great Rabbi has experienced that sense of holiness and purity. Moses was aware of the effect he had on the Jews and, therefore, wanted to give every Jew the opportunity to see his face. Even though he realized that he would be physically hard- pressed to judge alone, his tremendous *Chesed* and love for the Jewish People prevented him from denying them the chance to come face to face with him. Only a non Jew, Yitro, who didn't have that special quality of "*ahavat yisrael*" or "love for the people of Israel" could analyze the situation from a purely rational perspective and give the necessary advice.

YITRO – *Soul Seeing*

When the Jews were receiving the *Torah* at Mount Sinai the *Torah* says that they could "see the sounds" of the heavenly shofar blasts. "How can sound be seen?"

There are two approaches that are offered to answer this question. The first, cited by Rashi, is that God actually created a sound that could be seen by human eyes. It was a miraculous creation for a spectacular one time event.

The second answer is that God gave the Jews "super vision", enabling to see what normal human eyes cannot. It was as if God handed out 3D glasses to the people which they all put on and were suddenly able to see sound waves. According to this approach the sound stayed the same but their vision was miraculously enhanced.

I think there is a third approach that teaches us a powerful message. Neither the sound nor their vision was changed or enhanced in any miraculous or supernatural way. Instead, God removed the barriers or filters that cloud our normal vision. With those barriers gone, the people could actually see things that they could never have seen before.

Reflections

Just imagine if we could see every microscopic organism in the air around us. We'd probably go insane with the realization of being surrounded by billions of living things. Perhaps the reason we can't see those things is that our eyes have filters installed that act as barriers.

How many times do we see someone daily for months or even years and never pay serious attention to them and then one day, suddenly without warning, we see them in a totally different and more interesting light? Did they change or did you just begin to see things through a different, and possibly less rigid, filter?

The same holds true regarding spirituality. We can live through thousands of Saturdays and never feel anything special and then suddenly experience that same day through the lens of *Shabbat* and discover a world we never were able to see before, right there before our eyes.

They say that the eyes are the windows to the soul. When our eyes are all fogged up and blurred with distractions our soul can't always see to its full potential. When the Jews at Mt. Sinai had the barriers removed from their eyes they could see amazing things with their souls. We too need to remove the distractions blocking our eyes so that we can see the world through the pure and unencumbered lenses of our souls.

MISHPATIM – *Reincarnation*

The *Zohar* uses the beginning of this *Parsha* as the basis for a discussion regarding the reincarnation of the soul. According to the *Zohar*, a soul that has not completed its mission in its earthly lifetime can be sent back to this world in a different form to complete that mission.

The Maggid of Mezeritch asked the Baal Shem Tov, his teacher, why the *Zohar* chose this *Parsha* of *Mishpatim* to discuss reincarnation. The Baal Shem Tov told him to go to a certain hilltop overlooking a well and to observe until the evening. The Maggid found the hilltop and began observing the well. First, a wealthy merchant stopped by the well to rest and have his lunch. When he left to continue his journey the Maggid noticed that he had forgotten his wallet by the well. A little later another man stopped to eat at the well, found the wallet, and seeing no one around to claim it, took it and left. A short time later, a pauper stopped by the well to rest. After only a few minutes the first merchant returned to the well and began demanding his wallet from the pauper. When the pauper insisted that he knew nothing of a wallet the merchant beat him nearly to death. At this point the Maggid returned to the Baal Shem Tov.

The Baal Shem Tov explained that in a previous life the merchant and the second man were involved in a court case. The merchant was mistakenly declared the winner and was granted the sum of money that had been in his wallet, which really should have gone to the second man. The pauper had been the judge in the case, who had ruled incorrectly.

The Baal Shem Tov said that whenever we see a judgment that seems to be unjust we should have faith that it is really just the correction of an error made in a previous incarnation.

Reflections

The world can be a cruel place. Often, the wicked succeed while the righteous suffer. Divine justice is not always revealed to us, since our vision and understanding is limited. It is only faith in the Master of the World, who metes out absolute justice, which saves us from giving up hope in a better world.

MISHPATIM – *Servitude*

This *Parsha* opens with the laws related to indentured servitude. According to the law a Jew who was indentured into servitude to pay off a debt was only required to serve for a maximum of six years and was freed in the seventh. If, however, he chose to remain and serve his master indefinitely (defined by the Talmud as a maximum of fifty years) he would have his right ear pierced against a doorpost.

The reason for the six year maximum period reflects the idea behind the sabbatical year and the weekly *Shabbat*, testifying to God's mastery and ownership over the world. The Talmud explains the reason for the ear piercing as follows. The doorpost represents the Mezuzah, and that God saved the Jews from the plague of the first born in Egypt and set them free. By voluntarily choosing a prolonged term of servitude, that individual is also choosing a human master instead of God. The piercing of his ear against the doorpost castigates him for this choice and serves as a constant reminder of his rejection of God's mastery.

Reflections

While the practical aspects of these laws of servitude are no longer applicable, the ideas behind them are as relevant as ever. Many of us voluntarily enslave ourselves to our jobs and careers. Although pursuing material ambitions is not contrary to *Torah* teachings we must remember to always confine our "slavery" to six days and set ourselves free on the seventh, the *Shabbat*. By doing so, we can be certain never to trade our loyalty to God for loyalty to a human master. No matter how enslaved we might feel during the week we can all feel free on the *Shabbat* not only by not working, but by transforming our lives into spiritual and emotional fulfillment.

May we all be blessed to appreciate and experience *Shabbat* to its fullest potential.

TERUMAH – *Above and Below*

There are two ways that Divine Providence can affect, or interact with, the world. One way is for Divine Providence to emanate from the heavens without any prodding from the world "below". An example of this is the miracle of the splitting of the sea. According to the Talmud the Jewish People didn't merit a miracle. In fact they were hardly any holier that their Egyptian oppressors. God performed the miracle without any compelling reason from "below". The other way is for Divine Providence to be, so to speak, pulled down from below. An example of this is the miracle of Hanukah. The Jews formed an army and fought the Greeks and only then did God miraculously give them victory and freedom. The Jews "pulled down" the Divine Providence by starting the process of salvation themselves. The modern state of Israel might very well be another example of this idea of the Jews starting the process of salvation and, by doing so, pulling down the Divine salvation.

The revelation at Mt. Sinai was clearly an example of the first type of Divine Providence. God revealed Himself and the *Torah* to the Jewish People without any prodding from them. All they had to do was to be there and accept the revelation.

The *Mishkan* is an example of the second type of Divine Providence. By building the *Mishkan* and worshipping in it the Jews actively attempt to connect to the Divine and to bring the Divine Presence to dwell among the nation. The *Mishkan* then is certainly not a place for God to dwell in. Rather it is a vehicle for the Jewish People to "pull down" the Divine to dwell within each and every Jewish soul.

The Talmud calls the synagogue a "*mikdash mi-at*" or a small sanctuary. Just as the *Mishkan,* and later the Holy Temple in Jerusalem, was a vehicle for the Jews to "pull down" the Divine Presence so to is every synagogue a vehicle for the same. The synagogue is not "the" place where God dwells. God dwells everywhere or, as the Rebbe of Kotzk said, "God dwells wherever man lets him in". Rather, the synagogue is the most opportune place for Jews to connect to God through prayer. Through our prayers we can draw the Divine Presence to dwell among us.

TERUMAH – *Details*

In this *Parsha* of *Terumah* God commands the Jews to, "build for Me a *Mishkan* and I will dwell within you". The famous question on this verse points out that it should say, "and I will dwell within it". The answer given is that God doesn't dwell in a building but rather in the hearts of every person.

Why then do we need a *Mishkan* at all for God to dwell among us? The *Parsha* continues to describe in great detail all of the vessels and utensils needed to be built for the *Mishkan* such as the Ark, *Menorah*, Table, and even the smallest and most mundane things such as the curtains, covers, and the poles used to carry everything. Why are all these minute details necessary? Does God really care what color the curtains to the *Mishkan* are or exactly how large the *Menorah* is?

The *Mishkan* and its vessels are spiritual tools to help us connect with God. God gives Man the opportunity and the tools to influence the spiritual realm of Divine Providence. For example, the reason why we blow the shofar on the Day of Judgment is because it symbolizes the ram that Abraham sacrificed instead of Isaac, in the famous episode of the Binding of Isaac and, therefore, it symbolizes the mercy that God showed to spare Isaac. The blowing of the shofar on Rosh Hashanah mystically has the God given power to influence the Divine judgment towards mercy.

Every detail of the *Mishkan* has specific spiritual and mystical power to influence the Divine for the good of the world. For example, the Ark evokes blessings of spirituality, the *Menorah* blessings of wisdom, and the Table blessings of livelihood. The same is true for every vessel of the *Mishkan*, even the most seemingly insignificant. Therefore, the spirituality and blessings evoked through the *Mishkan* cause the Divine Presence to dwell among the Jewish People and bring light and blessings to the entire world. This also explains the great tragedy and darkness that the destruction and loss of the Temple in Jerusalem (the permanent *Mishkan*) brought, and continues to bring, to the world.

Just as the *Mishkan* and its vessels are spiritual tools to help us connect with God and influence the Divine realm so too are the *Mitzvot*. Every detail of every *Mitzvah* has a very specific spiritual and mystical power to influence the Divine for the good of the world. Each time we perform a *Mitzvah* we should be careful to try to perform it completely, according to all its details. In this way we will be able to influence the world of the Divine and bring special blessings upon us and the entire world.

TERUMAH – *Giving*

In this *Parsha* the Jews are asked to contribute towards the building of the *Mishkan,* and they respond so generously that Moses tells them to stop giving, when their target amount is reached and exceeded. Anyone who has ever done any fundraising knows that you never tell people to stop giving! There is always more good work that any extra money can be used for in the future, so why tell the Jews to stop giving?

There are two ways of giving. One way is to give because there is a need to fill. This form of giving is purely to help another. The only objective is to fulfill someone else's need. This is the highest form of giving.

Another form of giving is motivated by a need in the giver. Giving makes the giver feel good about himself. This is not necessarily a bad thing, but it is not the purest form of giving selflessly. For example, someone offers to set you up on a date with a particular person they like and, for personal reasons, you decline their offer. If they are acting solely to help you, they will not be insulted and will continue trying to set you up to help you find your true match. However, if they are focusing on making themselves feel good through their giving, they will be insulted and angry at your refusal to accept their generous offer. They might stop setting you up, and find someone else to "help" so as to satisfy their desire to feel good about themselves through giving.

Moses wanted to make sure that the Jews were giving solely for the purposes of building the *Mishkan* so that the building would be based on totally pure acts and intentions. Therefore, when the amounts need to build the *Mishkan* were collected he stopped fundraising. Once the needs of the *Mishkan* had been met any further giving would be solely to fulfill the need of the individual giving.

Reflections

The next time you find yourself in the position of "giver", stop and think. Why am I giving? Is it really only to help another, or is it to make myself feel better. It's ok if your answer is the latter, but it should motivate you to explore your motivations and objectives.

TEZAVEH – *In Style*

This *Parsha* describes, in minute detail, the garments worn by the Kohen while performing the service in the Temple. Why did the Kohen require special clothing to serve in the Temple?

According to the mystical and kabbalistic commentaries the priestly garments were precisely designed to evoke spiritual energies in the heavenly spheres. They provided the Kohen with the tools to successfully usher the prayers and offerings of Israel up to the highest reaches of the Divine realm.

In addition to their mystical role, the beauty and majesty of the Kohen dressed in the priestly garments evoked a sense of awe and pride in the people which helped them attain the proper state of mind in which to focus their prayers and offerings to God.

Aside from covering the head and the parts of the body deemed "immodest", there is no obligatory prayer uniform outside of the Temple in Jerusalem. However, just as the priestly garments were meant to instill awe and pride to help attain the proper state of mind when praying to God, so too should our own style of dress.

The way we dress clearly affects the way we feel and behave. Dress codes are established by companies, schools, and social events for that very reason. A business person dressed in a smart and professional looking suit has a much better chance of success not only due to the impression given off but because of the way that person thinks of himself, and the confidence that clothing helps to instill. The atmosphere at a "black tie" event is immediately enhanced and uplifted by the color and style of the clothing worn.

The same is true regarding our style of dress when praying. If we wear our everyday "hang out" clothing then we can only expect to feel like "hanging out" instead of the serious and thoughtful attitude required for prayer. On the other hand when we come to shul on a *Shabbat* morning dressed in our finest we feel as though we are taking part in a serious endeavor requiring our full attention. We are also showing respect for the place and for our fellow congregants.

When we pray we come before God, King of the Universe. Ask yourself this question. "How would I dress if I had to meet the President of the US or the Queen of England or even just a potential employer at an interview?" When you answer that question honestly you'll know what to wear when praying to God.

TEZAVEH – *Where's Moses?*

The *Parsha* of *Tezaveh* is the only *Parsha*, relating to a time after the birth of Moses, that does not have Moses' name within it. One of the explanations for this is that when pleading Israel's case Moses asked God to erase his name from the *Torah* rather than destroy his people to create a new nation from him. This *Parsha* is the fulfillment of that plea.

The primary content of *Tezaveh* relates to the clothing worn by the Kohen, specifically the High Priest, during the Temple service. God chose Aaron, Moses' brother, and his direct descendants to serve as High Priests for eternity. The Rabbis discuss the feelings of rejection that Moses undoubtedly felt at being passed over for the holiest of all positions. He certainly seemed qualified for the position. He was the greatest prophet ever to exist, having been the only man ever to come "face to face" with God. He was also the greatest leader, teacher, and overall spiritual personality. Why then was Moses passed over for the job?

The Talmud teaches that Aaron was involved in making peace between the Jewish people. To accomplish this he needed to be intensely involved in the everyday lives of the people, getting to know their strengths and weakness, and experiencing their triumphs and defeats. The job of the High Priest was to plead for the atonement of the people. To help them attain atonement he had to be able to understand their sins, experience their remorse, and show them the way to repentance. Aaron had the right experience for the job. Moses, however, was on such a high spiritual level that he had to remain separate from the people to maintain it. He couldn't be the one to plead for, and attain atonement for, the people. Therefore, Moses' name is left out of the *Parsha* as a show of sensitivity to his being passed over for the job.

KI-TISA – *Family Connections*

When God tells Moses that the Jews are worshipping the Golden Calf and that, as punishment, He will destroy them Moses pleads to save the nation. It is only after Moses "reminds" God of the promises He made to Abraham, Isaac, and Jacob that God causes His anger against the people to subside.

Here's an example that can help us understand how the merit of the forefathers, who lived hundreds of years before Sinai, was able to save the people from destruction. Imagine going on an important job interview. You're extremely nervous because you desperately need this job. You come into the boss's huge, imposing office and sit in a chair facing the distinguished looking executive with the power to "make or break you". Your heart is racing and your stomach feels like it's on a rollercoaster. The executive picks up your resume from a pile on his desk, glances at it, and then looks you straight in the eye. "Mr. Goldberg, I see that you are from Sacramento. Is your grandfather Sid Goldberg?" Surprised, you reply, "yes". Suddenly you see a huge smile cover the executives face. "I went to school with your grandfather. He was one of the most honest and upright people I've ever had the honor of knowing. If you are his grandson you must have learned from him". You breathe a sigh of relief, the interview goes smoothly, and you get the job.

We begin the Amidah, the prayer that represents our personal audience or "interview" with God, with the mention of Abraham, Isaac and Jacob. By "reminding" God that He knows our grandfathers we change the entire atmosphere of the interview. We are transformed from terrified strangers into grateful old friends or "*mishpocheh*" who can plead with God and ask Him anything without fear of rejection.

Our relation to our forefathers and their tremendous merit is what we rely on when we stand before God without sufficient merit of our own. By relating to them, by following in their ways, we tell God that since we are their descendents we also possess their great character traits and tremendous faith. In their merit, may God watch over us and grant us blessings.

KI-TISAH - *Artistic Spirit*

In this *Parsha* of *Ki-Tisah* God appoints Betzalel as chief architect and designer of the *Mishkan* and promises to fill him with a spirit of wisdom and creativity. In the previous two *Torah* portions God gives the Jews very specific instructions and specifications for building the *Mishkan*. The design and dimensions of all of the holy utensils as well as the clothing of the priests is clearly recorded. Why, then, does Betzalel require this special gift of wisdom and creativity to build the *Mishkan*? Isn't he required to follow the blueprint given to Him by God and clearly recorded in the *Torah*?

Betzalel absolutely had to follow the blueprint given to him by God but within that blueprint he had the opportunity to apply his own creativity to reflect the holiness within his soul and the souls of the Jewish people.

In the last "Halleluyah" psalm that we say every morning in our prayers, the psalmist extols the people to praise God with every sort of musical instrument and sound. The message is that prayer and praise doesn't have to be confined to words. The greatest form of prayer and praise is when a person does it by using his most precious and valuable talents, be it music, dance, writing, cooking, speaking etc. That's why prayer is called "service of the heart" and not "service of the lips", because prayer must reflect the innermost essence of a person, otherwise known as the soul. That soul is found in a person's creativity in whatever form that may take. That's also why no two prayers are alike; because no two souls are the same.

God gives us a way of life to follow in the *Torah* replete with do's, don'ts, and boundaries. It is our responsibility and privilege to use our individual creativity, within those boundaries, to make the *Torah* appealing to our own souls. Every soul has a unique path to spirituality and holiness and that path is formed and molded by our own creativity and talents. One person might connect with God through art, another through food, and another through sports. Since no two souls are the same, every person must apply their unique talents and creativity to discover or create their own unique path to God.

KI-TISA – *Counting*

The *Parsha* begins with a command to count the Jewish People by collecting a half shekel from each person. One reason for the required half shekel collection is because the *Torah* prohibits the direct counting of people. For example, when King David took a census by counting people instead of half shekels the people were punished with pestilence. What is the reason for this prohibition to count people?

To formulate an answer we first need to understand the significance of counting. Counting qualifies the unknown. The Talmud teaches that a person can test God's promise to reward those who give charity by increasing their wealth. However, this is only true if the person testing doesn't have an exact accounting of his money. If he has an exact count he can't expect that count to miraculously increase.

God promised our forefathers that He would make their offspring into a nation as numerous as the stars in the sky and the sand on the beach. By counting Jews we prevent that promise from being fulfilled.

Another way to understand the significance of counting is that it represents ownership. Only an owner is concerned with an exact counting of his possessions. Just as the laws of *Shmitah* and *Yovel* proclaim God's sole ownership of all of the land so too does the prohibition to count proclaim that all people belong to Him. To count people is to deny this truth and to attempt to replace God by proclaiming ourselves masters of ourselves and of our destinies. By collecting and counting a half shekel from each person we affirm our belief in God as master of the world.

VAYAKHEL – *Don't Light My Fire*

After repeating the command to observe the *Shabbat* the *Torah* specifies the prohibition of creating fire on *Shabbat*. Out of the thirty nine categories of activities prohibited on *Shabbat*, which are all derived in the Oral Law, why is creating fire the only one stated openly in the actual *Torah* text? The classic rabbinic commentaries offer several explanations.

Since fire was permitted in the Temple sacrificial service on *Shabbat* we might think that it was also permitted outside of the Temple. Therefore, the *Torah* teaches us that fire was forbidden outside of the Temple on *Shabbat*.

Another explanation is that since fire is permitted for cooking on the Festivals, which possess all of the other *Shabbat* prohibitions with the exception of carrying, we might think that creating fire for cooking on *Shabbat* is also permitted. Therefore, the *Torah* teaches us that creating fire on *Shabbat* is prohibited in all circumstances.

Finally, there is a special obligation to "enjoy" *Shabbat* (Oneg *Shabbat*). Since fire is the source of much of what gives our bodies enjoyment including heat, food, and light, we might assume that it is permitted on *Shabbat*. The *Torah*, therefore, takes special interest in teaching us not only that creating fire is, in fact, prohibited but that *Shabbat* "enjoyment" is defined differently than weekday enjoyment. The character of "Oneg *Shabbat*" is characterized by spirituality while weekday enjoyment is defined as physical. *Shabbat* enjoyment includes *Torah* study, singing, praying, festive meals, and connecting with friends and community. It does not include television, movies, workouts, and road trips, even though these activities make us happy on any other day.

The *Torah* teaches us to refrain from creating a physical fire on *Shabbat* and to, instead, create a spiritual fire in our hearts and souls with which to observe and enjoy the holy and spiritual day of *Shabbat*.

VAYAKHEL – *Shabbat & Community*

The first words of the *Parsha* tell us that Moses gathered the entire community of Israel together to address them regarding the *Shabbat*. This is the only time in the *Torah* where this language of gathering the community together (*vayakhel*) is used. Why then was this gathering necessary relating to the subject of *Shabbat*?

Shabbat observance is arguably the most important act of observance in Judaism and therefore it warranted a special communal gathering. Observance of the *Shabbat* is what typically categorizes someone as being observant of the *Mitzvot*.

A more direct connection between community and *Shabbat* is that although *Shabbat* observance is a personal obligation, in many respects, it can only be properly observed in a community. Joining other Jews to pray, study, sing, and eat is a large part of what makes *Shabbat* spiritually and emotionally fulfilling. While a *Shabbat* alone can be meaningful and fulfilling, it cannot approach the level of meaning and fulfillment attainable within a community.

There is one more reason why *Shabbat* observance is linked to community. Besides the importance of observing *Shabbat* "in" a community there is also the concept of observing *Shabbat* "as" a community. The Talmud teaches that if the entire nation of Israel would observe just two *Shabbat*s the Messiah would immediately come. There is, then, the unique and powerful notion of communal *Shabbat* observance in addition to individual observance. As in all communal initiatives, including prayer, the personal shortcomings of individuals are overwhelmed and nullified by the overall merit and observance of the community. The individual who lags behind in personal achievement can "ride on the coattails" of the community. This can only happen if that individual is part of the community.

Reflections

This is why it is so important to be part of a Jewish community not only in regards to *Shabbat* observance but also in all areas of our Jewish lives. When we are part of a community we no longer are "flying solo". Rather, we can depend on the support of the entire community to carry us through the challenging areas and times of our lives.

VAYAKHEL – *Shabbat Week*

The command to observe the *Shabbat* is almost always prefaced by the statement, "you shall do your work for six days etc." Why the need for this prologue related to the regular week? Why doesn't the *Torah* just tell us about the actual day of *Shabbat*?

One possible reason is that the *Torah* is making clear that it is an obligation to work. Whatever form that work takes it is an obligation for every person to use their talents, abilities, and creativity to help build civilization. By doing so, we become partners with God in Creation. When we observe *Shabbat* we emulate God by resting from creative activity. Therefore, by engaging in creative activity during the rest of the week we are emulating God's own creative acts.

Another way of answering our original question is that there needs to be a contrast between *Shabbat* and the rest of the week in order to make *Shabbat* stand out and appreciated by us. When we enter *Shabbat* from a busy work week we experience the spirituality and holiness of *Shabbat* much differently than if we enter *Shabbat* from the midst of a vacation. Therefore, by working during the week we are certain to appreciate *Shabbat* more fully.

There is one final answer that I think sheds a totally unique light on our understanding of *Shabbat*. *Shabbat* is not an isolated event in time. Rather, it is the climax of a process representing creation. That process begins on the first day of the week, crescendos in the middle, and climaxes on the seventh day, *Shabbat*. If *Shabbat* is part of a process then that process, and therefore *Shabbat*, is affected by what we do not only on *Shabbat* but also during the rest of the week. In other words, if *Shabbat* is 75% of the "process" and the rest of the week is 25%, we cannot reach a 100% level of fulfillment without both parts.

Based on this new understanding it is no longer possible to be a "holy" Jew on the *Shabbat* while acting dishonestly in business during the week for our weekday improprieties impinge upon our total fulfillment of *Shabbat*. We can't just be Jews one day a week. We need to imitate those Manhattan drug stores and be open 24/7 for *Torah* and *Mitzvah* observance. By doing so we will attain the wholeness and balance that will enhance our spiritual lives and contribute to our overall fulfillment.

VAYAKHEL – *One or Many?*

In this *Parsha* Moses gathers the people of Israel and tells them, "These are the things that God has commanded you to do". He follows this introduction by repeating the basic prohibition of work on *Shabbat* and gives the example of lighting a fire. The *Torah* continues with Moses once again telling the people, "This is the thing that God wants you to do", and goes on to describe the building of the *Mishkan* and its utensils.

There are many things that beg explanation in those first few lines of the *Parsha* discussed above. The question that I'd like to address is the use of the plural "these". Moses says, "These are the things that God has commanded you to do" but then only lists one thing: *Shabbat*. He should have said "this is the thing" just like he did a few lines later.

The answer, I think, can be found in a deep understanding of the incident of the Golden Calf in last week's *Parsha*. When the Jews made the golden calf they pointed to it and proclaimed, "These are your God Israel". They should have said, "This is your God Israel". Why did they use the plural?

Based on the commentaries it is pretty clear that the Jews did not intend to worship the actual golden calf as their God. Rather, they planned to use the calf as a representation of God that they could see, touch, and physically relate to. This, however, is exactly what idolatry is. The idol worshiper doesn't believe that a particular tree, for example, is actually a god. He believes that the tree represents a higher power represented by the image of a tree. The more he worships the tree, however, the more he begins to solely focus on the tree and forget about the higher power. Eventually, the idolater completely forgets about the true source of power and ends up worshiping the physical symbol of that power. The Golden Calf was made of the material wealth of the people who demanded a physical form to worship instead of the awesome spirituality handed to them. "These" represents the physical things that people worship such as wealth, beauty, and possessions. This is what the calf represented and that is why the plural "these" is used referring to it.

The *Shabbat* is the antidote to man's desire to worship material things. On *Shabbat* we focus solely on the spiritual. When we celebrate and observe *Shabbat* we are therefore fixing the sin of the Golden Calf by countering the "these are your God" with "these are the things" – the *Shabbat*.

Pekuday - *Role Playing*

The Book of Exodus ends with a description of Moses supervising the final tasks in the building of the *Mishkan*. With that completion Moses was henceforth prohibited from entering the holiest space in Judaism, the Holy of Holies in the *Mishkan*. Moses, the greatest prophet to ever live who spoke to God more directly than any human being had, or ever would, could not perform the Temple service. That job was given to Aaron and his descendents. Moses, then, was like a worker who spends months building a palace into which he is forbidden to enter once completed. How could Moses not have been upset and disappointed at this turn of events?

The Sages in the Ethics of Our Fathers teach that a rich man is one who his happy with his lot. This is the key to personal happiness. It's not what or how much you have, it's whether or not you're happy with what you have. There are people that have millions but are unhappy because they want hundreds of millions. Then there are those that have just what they need to survive but they are happy because their lives are fulfilled. Those who judge their success by comparing themselves to others will never feel totally fulfilled and successful because there will always be someone else out there who can do something better than them. For example, imagine listening to a concert given by a famous violinist and feeling like a failure because you can't, or probably will never, play the violin that well. With that attitude you would always feel like a failure in everything.

Moses could have felt like a failure after completing the *Mishkan* because he could no longer participate in the sacrificial service, but he didn't. Moses realized that everyone has their own unique role to fulfill in God's master plan.

We all need to identify our particular skills and talents and then work our hardest to use them to follow the ways of the *Torah* and to make the world a better place.

The Book

of

Vayikra

"Priestly Laws"

Vayikra – *From a Distance*

This *Parsha* begins with the words, "And He called out to Moses" followed by "And God spoke to Moses". The question is obvious. Why did God first "call out" and then "speak" to Moses? This is the only place in the *Torah* where God "calls out" to Moses. Why here?

Calling out implies distance. You call out to someone who is far away. When the Jews were taken out of Egypt they were all able to see God's presence in their midst. The Talmud teaches that at the splitting of the sea even the simplest Jewish maid servant was capable of seeing spiritual visions equal to those of the greatest prophets. God's presence permeated the Jewish camp. Every Jew saw the greatest revelation of God's presence at the giving of the *Torah* at Sinai. Then the Jews sinned with the Golden Calf. They didn't want to relate to God directly, or "face to face", as did Moses. It is only after the sin that God tells the Jews to construct a *Mishkan* to act as the central concentration of holiness. Moses supervises the building of the *Mishkan* but when it is completed he is not allowed to enter its holiest part or officiate in the sacrificial services because he is not a Kohane. With the completion of the *Mishkan*, at the end of the preceding *Parsha*, Moses feels a degree of distance and even rejection before God. Therefore God "calls out" to him, telling Moses that even though he thinks that he is distant he is not.

Based on what we said above the building of the *Mishkan* was, in a way, a sad event for it changed the very open relationship between God and the Jews and created certain barriers of entry or distance. In this week's *Parsha*, directly following the completion of the *Mishkan*, God gives the Jews the way to bridge that distance: the sacrificial offering.

Reflections

Feelings of existential distance usually result from the way we perceive ourselves. We tend to rate our own self worth against standards set by the society around us. Moses felt distant from God because he could no longer enter the sanctuary. God told him, however, that his closeness to Him was not tied to his physical inclusion in the Temple rite. Rather, his spiritual position depended solely on what was contained within his mind, heart, and soul. So too it is for each of us. Our feelings of self worth should not be dependant upon what kind of job we have, how much money we make, or how we look or dress. God judges us on who we really are by looking into the depths of our souls to find the real "us".

Think about this next time you rate yourself against someone else or judge your self worth based on the latest societal expectations.

Vᴀʏɪᴋʀᴀ – *Coming Closer*

The word "Korban" is commonly translated as sacrifice, and refers to the various offerings, animal, produce, or incense, that were offered upon the altar in the *Mishkan* and later in the Temple in Jerusalem. Sacrifice comes from "sacra", which means sacred or holy and "facere", which means to do or perform, in old French. Therefore, sacrifice literally means, "to perform a religious or holy act". Most of the pagan religious rituals revolved around animal and, in some cases, even human offerings, which is probably why the modern word sacrifice became associated with these offerings.

The accurate meaning of the word *Korban*, however, comes from the root word meaning "to come close". The purpose of the Temple offerings was to bring man closer to God.

How does one come close to another? By giving of oneself to the other. The very act of giving, which usually entails some sort of "sacrifice", as the word is commonly defined, shows the receiver that the giver is sincere in attempting to create a closer relationship with him.

In order to bring an offering in the Temple a person would have to first purchase the animal, which in those days would probably compare to buying a car today, and then bring it all the way up to Jerusalem where it would be offered by the Kohen. The very act of spending all that money, time, and effort for the sole purpose of fulfilling the *Torah* and serving God would, in and of itself, bring the person closer to God. Therefore, there is in fact a connection between Korban and sacrifice.

Today, when we have no Temple in Jerusalem and therefore no way to offer a Korban, how do we show our closeness and "sacrifice" to God? The Talmud teaches that since the destruction of the Temple the prayer service takes the place of the Temple service. Therefore, we pray three times a day to represent the three unique offering times in the Temple. But where is the sacrifice in our prayer? What do we sacrifice or give up when we pray? Granted, if everyone would have to pay, say, ten dollars to pray, then that would show some sacrifice. It also would probably leave synagogues very empty.

Rabbi J.B. Soloveitchik explains that in our private prayers, by asking God to provide us with all of our needs, including health, livelihood, shelter, and knowledge, we are giving up control over our lives and putting all of our trust in Him. We are sacrificing our control, Man's most precious and sought after commodity. By doing so, we become the Korban and bring ourselves closer to God.

Reflections

What an amazing concept. Man has the ability to get close to God simply by giving of himself. We should view every *Mitzvah* as an opportunity to give to He Who commanded us to perform it. Before performing a *Mitzvah* we should stop for a moment and gain the awareness that we are performing it solely because God commanded us to. By doing so, we demonstrate our subservience to God, thereby giving up our sense of control over our destiny. In this way, every *Mitzvah* we perform becomes a sacrificial offering – a Korban.

So many *mitzvot* relate to giving to others. Therefore, we can actually get close to God by caring for and about our fellow man. Every good deed we perform becomes a Korban.

SHMINI – *A Strange Fire*

The previous *Torah* portions record the completion of the *Mishkan* and the very detailed instructions given to Aaron and his sons explaining the specific method of performing each individual sacrifice. In this *Parsha* of *Shmini* Aaron offers the sacrifices as instructed and a heavenly fire devours the offerings in front of the entire Jewish people. The presence of God fills the area and the people experience one of the most spiritual ecstasies imaginable. At that moment two of Aaron's sons, Nadav and Avihu, get so caught up in the spiritual nirvana that they impulsively offer the holiest offering, the incense, on the altar. Instead of reaching the ultimate in holiness, however, Nadav and Avihu are themselves consumed by the heavenly fire.

What went wrong? Weren't Aaron's sons expressing their highest and holiest spiritual feelings by their actions? The *Torah* refers to the offering of Aaron's sons as an "Aish Zara" or "strange fire". A better translation would be a foreign or inappropriate fire. Although the spontaneous offering of Aaron's sons had the purest intentions attached to it, the offering was not part of the instruction given to Aaron by God. Therefore, it was against God's will.

Spirituality means closeness to God. The only way we can possibly know how to get close to God is by God telling us how to. God mapped out the specific ways of getting close to Him in the *Torah*. The *Torah* is the Jewish roadmap to spirituality. Forms of worship outside of the *Torah* might seem "spiritual" but, for a Jew, they are "*Aish Zara*" or strange, foreign fires. The only path for a Jew to take to achieve spirituality, closeness to God, is the *Torah*.

Aaron's sons thought that they could get even closer to God by inventing their own vehicle of spirituality. God's message to the Jewish people was swift and absolute. The only way of achieving true spirituality for a Jew is the *Torah* and every Jew needs to find his or her specific way within it to reach the ultimate goal of closeness to God.

Reflections

So many people speak of having amazing spiritual experiences outside of the boundaries of the *Torah*. How can that be?

Firstly, the *Torah* is only the Jewish path to spirituality. The Gentiles have their own paths to reaching God and can successfully achieve their own spirituality in different ways. The only requirement, based on the *Torah*, is that they shun idolatry. Therefore, any non idolatrous form of worship that seeks to achieve closeness to the Creator is totally acceptable for the Gentiles. They do not have to become Jewish to get close to God and to obtain their particular heavenly reward. This is, of course, in direct contract to the teachings of the other major religious that require everyone to follow their path in order to "get to heaven".

Secondly, there are spiritual experiences that are true and there are those that are false. For example, someone on a drug induced high will enter into states that can be perceived as spiritual. Clearly, these drug induced states cannot be counted as legitimate ways of getting closer to the Divine. They are simply false attempts that create the illusion of true closeness or spirituality. The Jewish path to spirituality is based on God's own instructions as related in the *Torah*. Everything else is simply "Aish Zarah", or strange fire which could superficially seem like the real thing but in reality is just a false illusion.

WHAT IS TUMAH?

Several *Torah* portions deal with the subject of *Tumah*. The term *Tumah* is commonly translated as "impure". This translation however is incorrect because it is based on the word "pure" which really doesn't have a basis in Judaism. The correct definition of *Tumah* is "unfit or unqualified". When something or someone becomes Tameh (the adjective form of *Tumah*) it becomes unfit or disqualified from engaging in certain ritual activities related to the Temple and can cause other things to become Tameh through contact or proximity. *Tumah* is in no way a reflection of the person's "purity" of heart, mind or soul and it is certainly not related to cleanliness.

What then is the nature of *Tumah* and why does it make the bearer unfit or disqualified from engaging in certain Temple activities? Almost all types of *Tumah* result from some form of contact with death. For example, a person who is in the same immediate area as a corpse becomes *Tameh*. Another, more subtle, example is that a woman who experiences menstruation becomes *Tameh* because of her contact with the (perfectly normal and healthy) destruction of potential life.

The nature of Man is to achieve control over his life and destiny. Man needs assurance that he will have food on the table, a place to sleep and clothing to wear. He wants to know what he will be doing tomorrow, in a week, a month, a year, and five years. He exercises, takes vitamins, and visits a doctor regularly to make sure that he will remain healthy. He works hard and saves money for the future. He raises children, forms friendships, and creates communities to provide him with continuity, protection, and love.

Man tries, and often succeeds, in controlling his destiny, but there is one thing that he cannot control: death. Death leaps out from the shadows and claims its' prey with no regard for Man's careful planning and control. Man is helpless in the face of death.

When Man faces death he loses his self confidence, pride, and sense of stability and control. Suddenly he realizes that he has no control in this world. He is shattered. His faith severely injured. Why bother planning, working, loving, and believing when it could all end at any moment in the blink of an eye? In this state of despair Man becomes unfit to perform the rituals of faith because there is no way that he can perform them with the proper intention, emotion, and faith. Man first needs to come to grips with his existence in this world and learn to accept that every moment is precious and worthwhile in and of itself. The state of *Tumah* gives Man the time he needs to reflect on the real purpose of life and to regain his faith. He can then reemerge as a new person focused on living a fulfilling life of faith, truth, and love.

Reflections

Immersion in a *Mikvah* is part of the process of spiritual renewal. The water symbolically washes away the doubts and conflicts that constantly test our faith. The numerical value of the root of the Hebrew word for water – *Yam* –is equal to fifty, which represents going beyond our nature. The letter *Mem*, which is the first and last letter of the word *Mayim* (water) is the numerical value of forty, which represents transition and metamorphosis.

There are many ways that we can rejuvenate ourselves throughout the day and thereby remove ourselves from the *Tumah* that we often find ourselves experiencing. A short walk in the park can work wonders. Taking a few moments to sit quietly and take deep, relaxing breaths is great too.

KEDOSHIM – *Imitation*

The second verse in the *Parsha* of *Kedoshim* says, "You should be holy, for I, God your God, am holy." Rashi explains that this command to be holy refers to separating from sins, primarily those relating to sexual misconduct. In other words, holiness can be found in places, and among people, that are distant from sin and sexual misconduct. According to Ramban a person can fulfill the letter of the law while transgressing the meaning behind the law, thereby destroying the "holiness" emanating or resulting from obeying the law. Therefore, Ramban explains that the command to be holy refers to performing the commandments with extra care, above and beyond the minimum required, thus preserving both the letter and the spirit of the law.

The *Torah* doesn't usually cite the reasons for *Mitzvot*. The reasons for some of them are obvious, such as the prohibitions to murder and rob, while others, such as *kashrut* and sacrifices, are mysteries. Why does the *Torah*, in our above cited verse, give "for I, God your God, am holy" as the reason for refraining from sins and sexual misconduct? Isn't the reason as obvious as those behind murder and robbery?

The unfortunate truth is that in our modern society many sins, especially those relating to sexual conduct, are not viewed as either morally or ethically wrong. In fact, these sins are often praised and glorified by the people and institutions that we look up to. Therefore, for us, the reasons behind these sins are not obvious and need to be enumerated.

Since our minds and consciousness cannot accept the moral and ethical foundations of these rules the *Torah* gives us another reason for understanding and obeying them. That reason is, "for I, God your God, am holy." By separating ourselves from sin we are actually emulating God, which is really the greatest form of honor and respect.

Reflections

Sinning entails desensitization. What's the difference what kind of food I eat or who I have a relationship with? It doesn't really matter, right? That desensitization is the opposite of holiness, which represents uniqueness and awareness. It's also related to self esteem. If I don't think that I am special and unique then I don't have to be careful about what I do and with whom I do it with. Who do I think I am anyway?

Imitating God means recognizing that we are special and unique, and reflecting that awareness in our actions.

KEDOSHIM – *Being Holy*

In the *Parsha* of *Kedoshim* the *Torah* commands us, "You should be *Kedoshim* (holy) because I, God, your God is *Kadosh* (holy)". What does being "Holy" entail? Rashi explains that it means distancing oneself from the sexual relationships forbidden by the *Torah*. According to this definition, however, the second part of the verse doesn't make sense. The verse makes an analogy between us and God. We should be holy because God is holy. Now, if holy means separation from forbidden sexual relationships how does the analogous equation resolve itself? Is God holy because He separates from forbidden sexual relationships? Obviously not. What, then, is *Kedusha* – Holiness, and how do we attain it?

There are two types of separation. There is separation by withdrawal and isolation, and there is separation by elevation and refinement. The separation expressed in holiness is of the latter variety. This separation occurs through a conscious decision by Man to be unique in his environment.

Man creates holiness. Man builds a Temple and makes it holy. Man makes an animal holy to serve as a sacrificial offering. Man sanctifies the holidays. Mankind, specifically the Jewish People, is given the opportunity and honor to serve as a partner to God to bring Holiness into the world. For example, every time we recite a blessing before eating we are elevating that food to a state of holiness. We elevate our workplace by dealing honestly there. We elevate our dinning room by serving guests and by sharing words of *Torah* with them. We elevate the mundane and make it unique and special.

The land of Israel and the *Shabbat* are called holy because they both create a space to enable the Jewish People to separate and elevate themselves, both physically and spiritually.

God is the ultimate unique, or one of a kind, entity. Therefore, we are commanded to also be holy, or unique, by separating from and elevating the forbidden and the mundane, and thereby bring holiness into the world.

Reflections

We all have the power and privilege to create holiness in our lives. Everything we do, no matter how seemingly mundane, can be transformed into something holy. All it takes is sensitivity and awareness. We make eating holy by making the effort to choose kosher food and by taking a moment before and after consuming it to thank God with a short blessing. We make our work holy by conducting ourselves with integrity and respect regardless of the circumstances and challenges. We make our personal lives holy by creating and nurturing loving and caring relationships.

EMOR – *The Kohen*

The *Parsha* of *Emor* teaches the laws relating to the Kohen. One of the most difficult laws for us to understand is the law that prohibits a handicapped Kohen from serving in the Temple. This obviously strikes us as discriminatory and insensitive to the physically challenged or deformed. Since we are all God's children, and no parent would ever discriminate against one of his children, there must be a deeper way of understanding this law. According to our tradition every law in the *Torah* is God given and applicable to all time periods and societies. It is our duty to study these laws in a direct and honest manner to understand their true meanings and to reveal their lessons and messages.

The role of the Kohen is to act as a messenger for the Jew who comes to worship in the Temple. The Kohen is not an intermediary. What's the difference? An intermediary is someone who actually takes possession of what you give him and then presents it to a third party in his own manner. For example, a real state broker is an intermediary in that he listens to the buyer's angry offer and presents it to the seller in a sweet and pleasant tone. He transmits the buyer's intentions but not the buyer's exact words or tone. An example of a messenger would be a translator who translates word for word in the most exact manner possible.

As a messenger, the Kohen must totally sacrifice his individuality and uniqueness. He must not direct attention to himself. He must be practically invisible, like the underground telephone lines that allow two people to speak to each other. The Kohen is there to allow the Jew to communicate directly, in his own words, with God. Therefore, a Kohen must not have any physical characteristics that would draw attention to him and compromise his role as invisible messenger.

Contrary to an attitude of insensitivity, the challenged Kohen cannot be a messenger in the Temple service because the tremendous outpouring of sensitivity and caring expressed towards him by the worshippers would negate his special role as messenger.

Let us all follow the words of the *Torah* and treat our physically challenged brothers and sisters with great sensitivity and caring.

EMOR – *True Nature*

The *Torah* recounts an episode where the son of a Jewish woman and Egyptian father gets into an altercation with another Jew and proceeds to blaspheme the Divine Name, a crime carrying with it the penalty of death. The episode begins with the word " *Vayetzey* – and he went out", referring to the son. The *Midrash* questions the reason for using the word "*Vayetzey*". Where did he go out from? One of the answers presented in the *Midrash* is that he went out from his world, which is commonly explained to mean that he removed himself from, or forfeited, his portion in the World to Come by committing this grave sin.

I think there is also another way to explain this Midrashic answer. When the *Midrash* says that "he went out from his world" it doesn't necessarily refer to the World to Come. "*Olamo* – his world" refers to his nature.

A person's nature is defined by his soul, which is intrinsically pure and holy. Therefore a person is naturally drawn towards purity and holiness. In order for a person to sin he must go against his nature, or go out of his world.

The Talmud relates a story of four sages who attempted to enter into the deepest mystical realms of spirituality, referred to by the acronym of *Pardes*. One of the sages, Elisha Ben Avuyah, became a heretic as a result of this spiritual journey gone awry, and would travel throughout the Land of Israel, transgressing all of the laws of the *Torah*. As a result of this he was given the name "*Acher* – the other". His former student Rabbi Meir would follow Acher around and beg him to repent, but *Acher* refused for the following reason. While riding his horse on Yom Kippur on the remains of the Holy of Holies in Jerusalem *Acher* heard a heavenly voice saying, "Repent my children who have strayed...*CHUTZ* – except for *Acher*." According to one Talmudic version *Acher* finally did repent at the end of his life. Didn't the heavenly voice say that he couldn't repent? What changed?

There are two ways to explain the word *CHUTZ*. The first is as "except for", which is what lead to *Acher* not repenting. The other translation of the word is "get out". According to this translation the heavenly voice was telling Elisha Ben Avuyah that the only way he could do *Teshuva* (repent) was if he "got out" of *Acher* – the other. As we explained above, every person has a pure soul that draws him to holiness and purity. In order to sin a person must overcome his nature and become another person. It is this other person that sins. The heavenly voice was telling Elisha Ben Avuyah that he would only be able to repent if he could leave *Acher* – his other sinning personality behind.

Reflections

Our challenge is to be able to allow our true natures, holy and pure, to develop and dominate our actions. When that "other" side of us starts acting out we need to bring our true self, which is momentarily shoved to the side, to the forefront. Eventually the "other one" will stop trying to take control, and finally leave for good.

BEHAR – *Master Plan*

One of the greatest challenges to personal faith is the idea that we are directly responsible for, and in control of, our financial situation. We work long hours, make good business decisions, find good partners, and invest astutely. When we succeed financially as a result of our deeds we feel proud of our achievements and confident in our "golden touch". We have become masters of our destiny through our talents, skills, and diligence. God is no longer in the picture.

I n *Behar* the *Torah* teaches two laws that address the above challenge. The law of Shmittah states that a farmer must leave his fields fallow for the entire seventh year. Any produce that grows in his field during the seventh year can be eaten by the poor, free of charge.

The law of *Yovel* states that on every fiftieth year all real estate reverts to its original owner. All real estate sales, therefore, are actually just long term leases of up to 49 years.

The reason for both of these laws is to show us that we are not really the owners of our land. Rather, God is the true owner and we are just gracious tenants. No matter how hard we work and how cleverly we negotiate, on the seventh and fiftieth years God reminds us that we don't really control our destiny. The world belongs to its Creator.

God decides who will ultimately prosper and fail. Although we are commanded to work hard and wisely for our sustenance when we succeed or fail we must recognize that we are part of a greater master plan.

If we are blessed to succeed we need to use our wealth and influence to help others because, in truth, all wealth belongs to God and we are just temporary tenants asked to watch over it.

Reflections

The story is told of a great Chassidic Rabbi who requested a massive contribution from a wealthy follower and a relatively large sum from a poor one. The poor man scrimped, saved, and borrowed until he was able to present the sum to his Rebbe. The rich man scoffed at the "chutzpah" of the request and instead presented the Rebbe with a substantial, yet smaller, donation. In a few years the fortunes of the two men had switched. The rich man became poor and the poor man rich. The former rich man complained to the Rebbe. He had always donated generously. Why did he deserve to lose his fortune? The Rebbe explained, "God gives me money to disburse to the needy. Until I need the money I place it in a bank. If I can't withdraw my money from a certain bank when needed, I must move it to another bank where I can withdraw at will.

We are all caretakers of the wealth that God grants us. We need to realize that that money is for us to use for doing good in the world and helping others. If we just think of ourselves then we are wasting an amazing gift and opportunity to fulfill our destiny.

BECHUKOTAI – *Faith*

The *Parsha* of *Bechukotai* contains two sections. The first describes the blessings and rewards the Jewish People will receive if they follow the laws of the *Torah*. The second enumerates the horrifying curses and punishments that will be suffered if they do not follow the *Torah*. Another condition for punishment is added to "not following the *Torah*". God says, "if you will relate to Me with '*keri*' then I will also relate to you with '*keri*', and mete out these terrible punishments." Isn't disregarding the *Torah* sufficient to require punishment? What is "*keri*"?

Keri comes from the word *mikreh*, which means "by chance" or "coincidence". God says that if you relate to Him in a manner of chance or coincidence, He will relate to you in the same way which will, in and of itself, be a curse and punishment.

To understand this concept we need to understand what faith in God really means. Believing in God means that we accept that there is a master who controls and guides everything in His creation. Everything that happens in the world has a specific part to play in that master plan. Every blade of grass, every ant, every sunrise, and every tear is part of a grand, epic, and ongoing production that we are all players in. Faith in God means that when something, God forbid, bad happens to us we recognize it as part of a greater picture that we cannot comprehend, and we accept it, albeit with sadness and disappointment, and move forward, with our faith in tact. Without faith we place ourselves in a cruel world of chance and coincidence where terrible things happen for absolutely no reason, where we have no control or no way of coping with our setbacks. Lack of faith magnifies every setback into despair and hopelessness. Why go on living in such a cruel and chaotic world?

God tells us that if we relate to Him and His world with the attitude that everything just happens by chance, without any order or purpose, we will suffer the most terrible curses and punishments, because every negative event will become an opportunity for despair. If we live in a world of chance, nothing we ever do can positively impact it. Committing the most horrific crimes is just as meaningful as doing acts of kindness. Nothing matters. This is the curse and punishment of living without faith.

BECHUKOTAI —*Secret Formula*

The *Parsha* opens with the verse, "If you will walk in the ways of My laws and observe My *Mitzvot* and perform them, then I will send you rain in the proper time." The message of this verse is that God will reward us for performing *Mitzvot*. Why, then, does the verse have to tell us about "walking in the ways of the law?" It should just tell us to perform the *Mitzvot*.

The *Torah*, in this short verse, gives us the secret formula for successfully performing *Mitzvot*. According to the commentaries, "walking in the ways of My laws" refers to diligence in *Torah* study. To "walk" in something means to delve deeply into its depths and hidden meanings. In order to fully appreciate a *Mitzvah,* one must study its technical details, as well as its deeper spiritual meaning and message. The *Midrash*, *Zohar*, and Kabbalistic and Chassidic commentators all attempt to unravel and explain the spiritual mysteries and meanings of each *Mitzvah*, giving the individual the opportunity to connect with the Divine through them. Therefore, the formula for successfully performing *Mitzvot* begins with an attempt to understand them in the deepest way.

What is the difference between observing (Lishmor) and performing (Laasot) *Mitzvot*? Before performing a *Mitzvah* a person must take a moment to gain an awareness of what he is about to do. This is Kavanah, the act of directing all of our thoughts and feelings towards the single objective of connecting with the Divine through the performance of a physical act: the *Mitzvah*. The holy ARI preceded every *Mitzvah* with the recitation of a specific formula to focus the mind on Divine spiritual unifications. Every person can device his own method of gaining proper awareness before performing a *Mitzvah*. For example, before reciting a blessing, one should take a few seconds to remain silent and think about what he is about to do and who he is about to bless. This will create an awareness of God that will give the person's verbal act spiritual significance and gravity. When one has studied the spiritual meaning of the *Mitzvah* and taken the time to gain proper awareness of it, he can then perform it in the most effective and spiritually beneficial manner. Study + Awareness + Physical Act = Successful *Mitzvah*.

The Book

of

Bamidbar

"Numbers"

BAMIDBAR – *Social Order*

The Book of *Bamidbar* is called "Numbers" because it deals with counting and organizing the Jewish people as they set out on their journey from Mount Sinai towards the Promised Land. The *Parsha* of *Bamidbar* begins by counting each individual, then each family and each tribe. Each tribe is given a flag, representing its unique character trait, and is then assigned to a grouping of three tribes. Each group is then assigned a specific marching position, either to the north, south, east, or west of the Holy Ark, which always traveled in the center of the formation.

It is unusual for the *Torah* to describe seemingly mundane procedural matters in such great detail. What lesson is the *Torah* teaching us here? I think the *Torah* is attempting to show us the different strata that make up the social order and that are required to build a successful society.

Individual
The individual is the foundation upon which the entire social order rests. Every individual is unique. This is why, the Talmud teaches, God created a single human: to teach us that no two individuals are exactly alike and that each is as precious as an entire world. Based on this every individual has the opportunity and responsibility to develop his or her own unique talents and gifts in order to find happiness and fulfillment.

Family
There is a limit to what an individual can achieve working alone. Besides limited time and resources an individual requires moral and emotional support to function successfully. The custom of visiting the house of a *Shiva,* and the institution of communal prayer are examples of this idea. Family and friends give the individual the support to achieve that which he could not do alone.

Tribe
Just like individuals, family units are also limited in what they can achieve without joining together with other families to form

communities. In a community families with the same basic goals and beliefs join together to work towards common goals while still retaining a degree of independence to allow different forms of self-expression within the larger framework of those shared goals and beliefs. Each tribe constituted a community.

Tribal Cooperation

The twelve tribes were divided into four groups of three. This teaches us that even a community must often join with other communities to accomplish its goals. The Jewish world is, today, filled with organizations such as the Orthodox Union, RCA, UJA etc. that unite communities that share common goals.

Around the Ark

Each of the four tribal groupings was positioned in a different direction surrounding the Holy Ark, teaching us an important lesson. Individuals, families, and communities can maintain unique positions regarding politics, religion, and social issues. There is one condition. In Judaism these divergent positions must be centered around the core beliefs of t h e *Torah*, contained within the Holy Ark. As long as the *Torah* remains in the "center" the varying opinions can agree to disagree. This room for differences is part of the beauty of *Torah* Judaism.

Reflections

Hillel, the great Talmudic sage, taught, "If I am not for myself then who is for me" and "Do not separate from the community". A person must take care of his own needs while also caring for the needs of the community. Self-centeredness is not a viable option in Judaism.

Naso – *Equal in the Eyes of God*

The *Torah* is careful not to use a single extraneous letter. The sages of the Talmud often learn complex laws from letters or words that seem superfluous. In the *Parsha* of *Naso* the *Torah* seems to break this steadfast rule.

As part of the dedication of the *Mishkan* the princes of all twelve tribes bring tribute offerings. The *Torah* records each of these offerings even though every prince brought exactly the same offering. The *Torah* repeats the same list twelve times.

Why not just list the names of the twelve princes followed by the description of a single offering?

The *Torah* is teaching an important lesson by repeating all twelve offerings. Even though each prince undoubtedly wanted to bring greater and more unique offerings to show their gratitude and joy for the *Mishkan*, God told them to bring the same offering because in His eyes they are all equal.

The *Torah* is teaching us that material wealth does not raise a person's status in the eyes of God. The material is irrelevant because it is not earned. Rather, it is granted to Man by God regardless of the effort that Man expends, even though it seems to us that there is a direct correlation between wealth and effort.

There are several other places where this idea of equality before God is illustrated. When the Jews are counted in a census each one is commanded to give a half shekel regardless of his wealth. Rich and poor are equal. No matter how much a farmer wants to succeed in his agricultural endeavors every seventh year he must stop and leave his fields fallow in order to recognize that the land is not really his but rather belongs to God. Even in the world of real estate the greatest land deal is only temporary because in the fiftieth year all deals revert to their original owners. God once again is pointing out that the land really belongs to Him alone.

Reflections

Our society is fixated on honoring the material. We drink of the wisdom of Donald Trump and Warren Buffet and compile honored lists of the richest people. We all dream of being rich. Do we also honor the social workers helping the poor and needy and the volunteers manning the soup kitchens and shelters? Do we respect those that study *Torah* and perform the commandments as much as we respect those that succeed in the stock market?

After our 120 years in this world are completed, what will we be able to take with us and look back upon? If all we will have are material possessions and achievements then we will have absolutely nothing. The *Torah* portion is teaching us that we are all equal in the eyes of God when it comes to material things. If God does give us wealth we must use it to help others according the teachings of our tradition. We need to begin looking at others without judging them based on the material. We need to treat every person with respect regardless of what they do or how much they make. If we do this, then God will surely overlook our many faults and treat us with kindness and blessings.

BAHALOTCHA – *What Could Have Been*

The *Parsha* of *Bahalotcha* contains the two verses recited in the liturgy when the *Torah* is taken out and returned to the ark. These verses, "When the Ark went forth Moses said, 'Arise God and scatter your enemies. Let those that hate you flee from before You'. When it came to rest he said, 'Return God the myriads and thousands of Israel.' ", are preceded and followed, in the *Torah* scroll, by inverted letters Nun. This punctuation is not found anywhere else in the *Torah*. Why is it here, and what does it mean?

Rashi cites a *Midrash* that explains that the verses really do not belong in this particular place in the *Torah* but they were placed there to separate the preceding sin (leaving Mt. Sinai in excessive haste) from the following sin (the complaints for meat). The inverted Nuns point out this contextual misplacement.

Rabbi J.B. Soloveitchik explains that the two verses represent an alternate ending to the story of the Exodus. In fact, the verses represent the way that the story should have ended. The Jews had received the *Torah* and completed the *Mishkan*. God commanded them to assemble in marching formation around the *Mishkan* by tribe and flag. They were all counted, assembled, and ready to march into the Holy Land. The trumpets were blown, the formations set and the entire nation of Israel prepared to move out on their final journey to redemption. The Messianic age was at hand. "When the Ark went forth Moses said, 'Arise God and scatter your enemies. Let those that hate you flee from before You'. When it came to rest he said, 'Return God the myriads and thousands of Israel." These two verses could have described the final redemption. Instead the Jews sinned by complaining about meat and thus lost the chance to enter the Messianic age. The inverted Nuns highlight what could have been but what instead became "out of place".

Reflections

How often do we look back at events and wonder "what could have been" if we had just acted differently? We all have many different endings to our own stories. It's up to us to determine which ones will be actualized and which ones will remain in parentheses, out of place. May God give us the wisdom and courage to make the right decisions and choose the right ending.

BAHALOTCHA – *The Menorah – I*

The verse at the beginning of the *Parsha* tells us that, after receiving the command to light the *Menorah*, Aaron did exactly as he was commanded by Moses. Why would we ever think otherwise? Furthermore, the *Parsha* also says that God showed Moses a vision of the *Menorah* to serve as a blueprint. Why did Moses require a picture of the *Menorah* as opposed to any of the other holy vessels constructed for the *Mishkan*?

The *Torah* includes the written and oral laws, both of which were given to the Jews at Sinai. The oral law is transmitted from teacher to student in a continuous and unbroken chain stretching back to Sinai. One of the core beliefs in Judaism is that the oral law transmitted throughout the generations is fundamentally the same one given to Moses at Sinai. As we established previously, the *Menorah* represents the study and teaching of *Torah*. Just as the picture of the *Menorah* shown to Moses insured that the actual *Menorah* would be identical to that picture, so too is the oral law, represented by that *Menorah*, an identical copy of what was taught to Moses at Sinai. Aaron recognized and accepted this and, therefore, did exactly as he was commanded without modifying a thing.

BAHALOTCHA – *The Menorah – II*

The *Parsha* of *Bahalotcha* begins with the commandment given to Aaron to light the *Menorah* in the *Mishkan*. This immediately follows the description of the gifts that the princes of the tribes of Israel offered at the dedication of the *Mishkan*. The *Midrash*, cited by Rashi, explains the reason for this juxtaposition as follows. Aaron, who was the prince of the tribe of Levi, was not commanded to bring a gift for the dedication of the *Mishkan* and, therefore, felt slighted and inferior to the other princes. God then gave him the command to light the *Menorah* daily, implying that it is a much greater honor than a one-time gift.

This is an important lesson for it teaches the importance of consistency. This lesson manifests itself in the halachic principle of "*tadir v'sheayno tadir tadir kodem*", which loosely translated means that a *Mitzvah* that is performed on a regular basis takes precedence over one that only occurs occasionally. Another example relates to giving Tzdakah-Charity, where it is better to give a small amount each day rather than the entire amount at one time. The reason is because the spiritual effects of performing a "one time" *Mitzvah* wear off, while the performance of a *Mitzvah* regularly keeps those spiritual benefits fresh and active.

According to Jewish mystical teachings the *Menorah* in the *Mishkan*, and later in the Temple, represented the teaching and study of *Torah*, the light of the world. The Talmud teaches that the study of *Torah* is equivalent to all other *Mitzvot*. One possible reason for this is as follows. One of the main purposes of our lives is to bring ourselves closer to God. This closeness can be described as "spirituality". When we perform *Mitzvot* we achieve a degree of spirituality, but it is temporary. When we stop doing the *Mitzvot*, the spirituality ends soon after.

The study of *Torah*, however, is an all-encompassing experience that engulfs and immerses both our mind and soul. *Torah* study is not a temporary *Mitzvah*. We are commanded to study it day and night. Every moment of our lives is taken up with either studying or practicing the words of the *Torah*. Therefore, although the *Mitzvot* are all temporary vehicles to reach spirituality, the study of *Torah* is constant and all-encompassing.

The study and teaching of *Torah*, represented by the *Menorah*, is greater than the material gifts of the princes of Israel. Without it, the purpose of the Jews as a people, and of the entire world as God's creation, cannot be fulfilled. Therefore, Aaron was appeased when he received the *Menorah* as his lot.

Reflections

It's easy to get excited about a big new event or project. It's much more challenging to get excited about a task performed daily. The grand opening of a new hospital wing is cause for celebration, but visiting the sick on a daily basis is not usually the cause of celebration. Which is more important? The *Torah* teaches that it's the latter.

BAHALOTCHA – *The Menorah – III*

The word that is used to indicate the kindling of the flame in the *Menorah* is "*Bahalotcha*". Translated, the word means "when you will raise". Why didn't the *Torah* use a word which means "when you will kindle"?

Rashi cites two answers found in the Talmud. One answer is that the use of the word meaning "to raise" teaches us that there was a requirement to place a small stepping stool in front of the *Menorah* upon which Aaron would step on when lighting the *Menorah*. This requirement is strange for two reasons. Firstly, the *Menorah* was not so high as to prevent Aaron from reaching it without a foot stool. Secondly, even if it was a little too high why couldn't Aaron just use a longer stick to kindle the flame instead of a stool?

As we established previously, the *Menorah* represented the study and teaching of *Torah*. In order to be successful at *Torah* a student must make an effort to study it. The student cannot just sit back and wait for *Torah* knowledge to come to him. The student must take a step. He must go out of his normal, comfortable routine to seek out *Torah* and to study it. There is no shortcut to *Torah* knowledge.

The *Mishnah* in *Pirkei Avot* describes the way of *Torah* study as involving major physical and material sacrifice. In the great societies that we live in we are lucky not to have to make such sacrifices to study *Torah*. However, there are still sacrifices that to us might seem great, which must be made to acquire *Torah*. These might be as trivial as giving up an hour of television or gym time, taking a significant time off from work, or even leaving our homes to travel to a place of *Torah*. Without the effort, however, *Torah* cannot be acquired. This is the message of the stepping stool in front of the *Menorah*.

The other answer that Rashi cites in response to our original question regarding the use of the word "to raise" instead of "to kindle" is as follows. Aaron was commanded not only to kindle the *Menorah* but to make sure that the lights were capable of rising on their own power after the initial kindling was completed.

Reflections

The ultimate goal of any teacher is to become almost superfluous to the students further education. A teacher of *Torah* gives his students the tools required for independent study. He teaches them how to study a page of Talmud so that they can delve into any page of Talmud on their own and derive the laws and principles of Judaism therein. The teacher lights the flame of *Torah* in the student and remains on hand until the student can sustain, and expand, that flame independently.

SHLACH – *Never Despair*

In the *Parsha* of *Shlach* the Jews send the leaders of the tribes to scout the land of Israel. The scouts return with discouraging reports of the strength of the inhabitants and the inhospitableness of the land. Only two of the scouts, Caleb and Joshua, try to encourage the people with positive reports. The people ignore them and, believing the other scouts, become terrified of entering the Land and cry for the entire night. Because of this God punishes them by condemning them to wander in the desert for 40 years until a new generation can emerge to enter Israel. In addition the Talmud teaches that in response to the people's crying God said that since they cried on that night for no good reason He would give them a reason in the future to cry on that night, the ninth day of Av (Tisha B'av).

Why were the Jews punished so severely for crying? Is it wrong to cry? Although being in good spirits and serving God with joy is a basic principle of Judaism, so too is sadness and mourning at the appropriate time and situation. A person who is never sad or never cries is not normal! What made this crying different?

The *Parsha* recounts that when the people cried they also bemoaned their hopeless fate. The Jewish crying on that fateful night was not out of anxiety, fear, or even sadness. It was a crying of despair. On that night the Jews lost their faith in God and fell into a state of utter despair. They could see no reason to go on living in their situation. They even went so far as to yearn for the life of slavery and bondage they had just been freed from.

A Jew must never despair. He can cry, scream, beg, and plead with God for help but he cannot lose his faith. Without faith there is only despair, and God taught the Jewish people on that fateful night that despair is wrong, even unforgivable.

Reflections

I often wonder how Jews in the concentration camps, in the Ghettos, and in the hiding places of Nazi Europe managed to survive and eventually rebuild their lives. The answer is that those that survived never lost hope. They were determined to survive the horror and to live again. Despair and loss of all hope usually was followed closely by death. Nothing that we can even imagine can ever come close to the horrors of the Holocaust. What right then do we have to despair?

The lesson of *Shlach* is that despair is not an option. If we despair we condemn ourselves to wander in a wilderness of our own making with no way out. We must cry, scream, plead, and beg God to help but we must never despair. No matter how dark it looks there is always a light just around the corner.

SHLACH – *Shabbat Observance*

Towards the end of the *Parsha* the *Torah* recounts the incident of a man who is caught gathering wood on *Shabbat*, in violation of the prohibitions to gather and to carry in the public domain on *Shabbat*. According to the *Midrash,* the man is brought before Moses and the Sanhedrin (Supreme Court), who rule that the man had been given proper warning and that the witnesses to the act were qualified to testify in the matter. Then something strange happens. Instead of sentencing the man to death by stoning, as is required by *Torah* law, Moses, the court, and the entire community begin to weep. According to the commentators, they wept out of confusion and frustration because no one, including Moses, remembered the law regarding *Shabbat* violation.

Moses was forced to ask God to remind him of the law, after which the man was duly executed.

How could Moses and the people forget the laws regarding the *Shabbat* that they had received at Sinai just a few months before? It seems unlikely that Moses, the greatest teacher and prophet ever to have lived would forget such a basic *Torah* law. What, then, is really going on in this unusual episode?

I don't think that Moses and the Jews forgot the law. Then what was the reason for the confusion and weeping? Although they had studied and knew the laws of the *Torah*, especially the *Shabbat*, they had never actually had the practical need to deal with a transgressor. It is great to celebrate the *Shabbat* with festive meals filled with singing and words of *Torah*, long afternoon naps, and time spent with family and friends. But what about the prohibitions? What happens if someone makes a tiny fire on *Shabbat*, perhaps by just flicking a switch? Is that really a violation deserving of the death penalty? I can understand how murder might warrant the death penalty, but flicking a switch? It sounds outrageous and impossible.

This is what the Jews experienced. They knew that the man caught gathering branches was liable to the death penalty but they were shocked and overwhelmed by the prospect of actually putting the penalty into effect for a seemingly minor and harmless act. Moses didn't feel that the Jews would accept his explanation, that even a minor violation of the laws of *Shabbat* is actually a denial of the existence of the Creator who created for six days and rested on the seventh. He wanted them to hear it from God. After hearing the law from God the Jews understood the gravity of the offence and accepted, and carried out, the verdict.

Never again did the Jews question the importance of every law in the *Torah* and the penalties associated with them.

KORACH – *A Fitting Punishment?*

This *Parsha* recounts the story of the rebellion led by Korach and the 250 prominent Jewish leaders that joined him. In the end God punishes Korach and his followers in different ways. The earth opens up beneath Korach and his immediate family, devouring them and their possessions, and a fire comes down from heaven and devours the 250 followers. Why the different punishments? The *Mishnah* (Pirkei Avot) teaches that the opening of the earth was actually one of the things prepared during the final moments of the sixth day of creation. What is the significance of this and how does it relate to Korach?

Although on the surface Korach's grievances were against Moses and Aaron's leadership the commentaries explain that the rebellion was really against the validity of the *Torah*. According to Rabbi J.B. Soloveitchik it was a "common sense" rebellion, meaning that Korach wanted to create a Judaism based not on divine revelation and *Torah,* but rather on common sense. If something makes sense, do it. The purpose of this philosophy was to destroy the belief in a set of laws and commandments given directly by God. If a law is divine it must be adhered to in all circumstances even if it doesn't seem to make sense. Korach said that the law must solely be developed and guided by common sense, not divine fiat.

The Kabbalah teaches that God created the world to give to it and to allow mankind to draw close to Him. The Jewish path for drawing close to God is the *Torah*. In it God reveals to us the way to Godliness and Holiness through *mitzvot* and moral teachings.

Without the *Torah* there is no way to fulfill the purpose of creation: getting close to God. By rejecting the divinity of the *Torah*, Korach attempted to overturn the very purpose of creation. Therefore, Korach's punishment had to come from something that itself represented God's creation. The opening of the earth, according to the Talmud, was that vehicle.

The 250 followers of Korach were just that: followers. They did not originate the common sense philosophy nor did they necessarily espouse it as faith. They just joined the rebellion to follow a charismatic leader and to gain glory for themselves. They did not reject God. They just disobeyed Him. Therefore, the followers of Korach were punished in the same way as the son's of Aaron who offered the "strange" or inappropriate offering in the *Mishkan*.

Reflections

Common sense is a good thing when combined with faith in God. Alone common sense can, and has, led mankind down the road of error, misfortune, and even tragedy. Let's make it our mission to use our common sense to enhance our relationship with God through *Torah* and *Mitzvot*.

KORACH – *Tzizit*

The *Torah* commands us to put *Tzizit*, with one blue string included in each group of white strings, on each corner of a four cornered garment. The blue string is supposed to direct our thoughts towards heaven. According to the *Midrash* Korach instigated his rebellion by asking Moses the following theoretical halachic question. If an entire garment is blue does it require *Tzizit*? After all, if one blue string makes us think of heaven wouldn't an entire blue garment be more than sufficient without the need for an extra string?

The *Torah* completes the *Parsha* of *Shlach*, directly preceding Korach, with the *Mitzvah* of *Tzizit*. There must, therefore, be strong significance for why Korach used *Tzizit* as part of his argument and why the *Mitzvah* is then stressed in juxtaposition to the story of the rebellion.

The white strings of the *Tzizit* represent the 613 *Mitzvot* and the blue string represents the realm of the Divine. Korach argued that since every Jew is intrinsically holy he had no need for the *Mitzvot*. He could connect directly with the Divine without them. When Korach used the example of the completely blue garment he was referring to the Jewish people who are completely holy. He claimed that a blue garment had no need for *Tzizit*, just as the Jews had no need for the actual *Mitzvot*.

The *Torah*'s response to Korach is the very *Mitzvah* that he used to mock Moses with. Just as *Tzizit* require both the white and blue strings so too Judaism requires a combination of outer *Mitzvot* and inner spirituality. One cannot exist without the other. There can be no authentic Jewish spirituality without the *Mitzvot*.

The *Mitzvot* can be viewed as the physical keys that unlock the spiritual. A performed *Mitzvah* triggers an appropriate spiritual reaction. The only way to access that particular spiritual energy and force is via the performance of its corresponding *Mitzvah*. Therefore, only through the *mitzvot* can a Jew properly access spirituality and rise to spiritual heights.

Reflections

There are many different paths to reach spirituality and closeness to God. The Jewish path is through the *Torah* and *Mitzvot*.

CHUKAT – *Always On*

The *Parsha* of *Chukat* recounts one of the most incredible and tragic episodes of the Bible. As part of their punishment for the sin of the spies, the Jews begin their wanderings in the desert and immediately complain about their lack of water. Moses and Aaron pray for guidance and God responds by telling them to take the staff used by Moses to perform miracles and to verbally command a particular rock to produce water. Moses and Aaron approach the rock, in the presence of the entire nation, but instead of speaking to it they hit it twice, causing it to produce an abundant supply of water. God rebukes them for not having sufficient faith in Him and for not sanctifying Him in the eyes of the nation by simply speaking to the rock. God then punishes Moses and Aaron by denying them the right to entire the land of Israel.

This episode raises several difficult questions. It is impossible to imagine a harsher punishment than to deny the leaders of Israel the chance to realize the ultimate goal of their struggles and sacrifices. Why such a harsh punishment for simply hitting the stone instead of speaking to it? The Jews still witnessed a miraculous event! When God rebukes Moses and Aaron he tells them that their punishment is both because they didn't have faith in Him and because they didn't cause His Name to be sanctified before the nation. Can we actually believe that the two greatest figures in Jewish history lacked sufficient faith in God? Not likely. In fact the commentaries seem to say that they actually misinterpreted God's instructions and therefore hit the rock not in willful disregard of the command but rather in the belief that they were doing the right thing. The reason for their harsh punishment therefore must be because they didn't sanctify the Name of God before the people. Even though they caused a miracle to occur, to the joy and amazement of the nation, how much greater of a miracle would it have been had they produced the water by just speaking?

The *Torah* is teaching us a tremendously significant lesson. It's not enough to go through the motions and actions of Judaism. As Jews we each have the obligation to represent our faith in the most positive way. Our faith requires us to sanctify the Name of God wherever we go in whatever we do. Moses and Aaron failed in this task ever so subtly but because of their great stature were punished in the harshest way.

Reflections

We must think of ourselves as God's PR agency and try to take every opportunity to portray ourselves and our faith in the most positive light possible so that anyone seeing us will look upon us, and our God, with pride and honor. This is the meaning of the term, "*Kiddush Hashem*" or sanctifying the Name of God. The opposite of this is "*Chillul Hashem*" or desecration of the Name. The punishment for *Chillul Hashem* is considered to be almost unforgivable. The reward for *Kiddush Hashem* is immeasurable. Every time a Jew is in public he has the opportunity to create either a *Kiddush* or *Chillul Hashem* with his actions and behavior. It's a great responsibility that should constantly be in our thoughts as we navigate through our lives.

CHUKAT – *Reasons*

The *Parsha* begins by telling us that the law that will subsequently be described is a *Chok*, meaning that it has no discernable reason. It then describes the law of sprinkling the ashes of a Red Heifer upon someone who has come into contact with a corpse. While the ashes serve to purify the person being sprinkled they cause the person sprinkling them to become impure. This is clearly the ultimate example of a law without logical reason. Why, then, does the *Torah* have to precede the law with a caveat describing it as a *Chok*?

Rashi cites the *Midrash* that teaches that it is forbidden to try to come up with reasons to explain a *Chok*. Why would it be forbidden to simply think of reasons? Doesn't Judaism espouse intellectual investigation and speculation?

There are things in the world that are mysteries that we will never be able to comprehend. When we attempt to explain them with rational thought we will not find a satisfactory solution. At this point many will get discouraged and disillusioned. They will feel like abandoning their faith. Therefore, the *Parsha* tells us up front that there is a concept called *Chok* that will never be able to be understood. The *Midrash* clarifies further by telling us to not even try to find answers, because we will fail and then run the risk of losing faith.

Reflections

These mysteries, *Chukim*, prevent many people from believing in God and Judaism. They get stuck on a point, for which there is no satisfactory explanation, and cannot move forward. One example of this is the Holocaust. There is absolutely no satisfactory explanation as to why a tragedy of such enormous scope and evil could happen under the watchful gaze of the Almighty. It is a mystery. Those who demand an answer in order to believe in God will never get it, because there is none. They will remain stuck in the quagmire of doubt. The only way to move past this is to accept that there is a mystery that is troubling, but cannot be explained, and to continue exploring and searching to understand the parts of Judaism, God, and life that are fathomable.

Cʜᴜᴋᴀᴛ – *Faith Required*

In the *Parsha* Moses and Aaron are commanded, by God, to speak to the rock in order to draw water from it. Instead, they hit the rock to draw water and are punished with not being allowed to enter the land of Israel. The Talmud teaches that God's punishments are directly related to the sins committed. What, then, is the correlation between hitting the rock and denial of entry into the land of Israel?

After Moses and Aaron hit the rock God scolded them by saying that they lost the opportunity to sanctify (make holy – *kodesh*) His name before the nation. The Land of Israel is called the Holy Land. Its purpose is to help the Jewish nation to become sanctified and holy and thereby, sanctify the Name of God. By not sanctifying God's Name at the rock Moses and Aaron lost the opportunity to be in the land whose sole purpose is to sanctify His Name. This is also why the

Torah warns that if the Jews sin by following in the idolatrous and immoral ways of the nations the Land of Israel will vomit them out into exile. Only a holy people deserve to live, long term, in the holy land.

Another answer to our question is as follows. The essence of the sin of hitting the rock was lack of faith. Moses and Aaron should have trusted that just speaking to the rock would draw water as God promised. By hitting the rock they showed that they didn't believe strongly enough.

The Land of Israel has few natural resources. It is totally dependent on rainfall for sustenance. It is also surrounded by enemies sworn to destroy it. Only a person with tremendous faith can live in such a difficult land. The fact that it practically forces its inhabitants to have faith in God is exactly what makes Israel a holy land. Moses and Aaron lost the chance to live in this land of faith by acting in a manner that lacked faith.

CHUKAT – *Against all Logic*

In this *Parsha* we are presented with the concept of "*Chok*". A *Chok* is a *Torah* law that has no apparent logical reason attached to it. Rashi, citing a *Midrash*, says that a *Chok* is like a royal decree and therefore it is forbidden to question it or even to think about it. Does this mean that we shouldn't try to understand the meaning behind these *Mitzvot*?

One way of understanding this *Midrashic* teaching quoted by Rashi is as follows. There are many reasons for every *Mitzvah*, most of which are beyond our comprehension due to our limited spiritual capacity and world view. If we attempt to apply reasons to *Mitzvot*, when these reasons are proven incorrect we may lose faith in them completely. For example, assume that the reason for not eating milk and meat together is because that combination is unhealthy. Now that modern medicine has disproved this theory we should logically abandon this *Mitzvah*. This would be a tragic error on our part since the true reasons for the *Mitzvah* are far beyond our understanding, including even the scientific realm. Regarding our example, perhaps in a hundred years, more advanced scientific techniques will prove that milk and meat is, in fact, a harmful combination. Therefore, the *Midrash* is teaching that any reasons we might come up with to explain a *Chok* are inadequate and might lead us to erroneously abandon them.

There is another way to explain our *Midrash*. The *Midrash* isn't telling us not to think about the reasons for the *Mitzvot*. It is telling us not to solely think rationally or intuitively about them. The *Torah* and *Mitzvot* are not rational or intuitive rules and manners that we follow when they make sense to us. The *Torah* and *Mitzvot* are the word of God given to us to cherish and follow whether they make sense to our simple, human minds or not. Judaism is not about doing what makes sense or feels good. It is about elevating the holy soul that is within each of us, to higher levels of spirituality and closeness to God through the observance of the *Torah* and the *Mitzvot*.

It's not rational to take off time from work, and possibly jeopardize our career success, for the Jewish holidays or to leave early on a Friday when *Shabbat* starts at 4:30pm. It's not intuitive to get up early on Saturday morning to be on time for services. It's not rational to take a sandwich to work or on a road trip when there are so many great non-kosher places to eat at. It's not rational to not use a cell phone, PDA, Blackberry, computer, TV, VCR or DVD on *Shabbat*. It's not intuitive to pass up the best looking, smartest, most sensitive and romantic guy or girl you ever met just because they're not Jewish. It's not rational for Jews, who could live wonderful lives in Long Island, Manhattan, LA, or Miami to live in a tiny country in the Middle East surrounded by hundreds of millions of hostile enemies sworn to destroy them. It's not rational to take time off to study *Torah*. Most people think it's crazy, a waste of time. It's not going to help you make money, advance your career, or even look better or be healthier. However, if you want to grow as a Jew you must take the time to learn as much as you can. That means setting aside real time, not just five or ten minutes a day. It also means finding a teacher who has the knowledge and ability to pass along the great tradition (*mesorah*) of *Torah* to you.

Reflections

Once, a small boy trying to sneak into class ran into the Lubavitcher Rebbe, ZT"L. The Rebbe asked him where he had been and the student told him that he had gone to a baseball game and had left early when his team was down by 5 runs in the final innings. The Rebbe asked him if he had learned anything from the game and when the boy remained silent the Rebbe explained as follows. Each team has nine players that play the game and there are thousands of fans that watch. As long as their team is doing well the fans cheer. However, when things look hopeless the fans give up and leave but the players all stay until the end, no matter what. That's the difference between a fan and a player.

Join the team. It's not logical. It doesn't make sense. People might even laugh at you at think you're crazy. But if you want to grow as a Jew I believe that it will be the best and most rewarding decision you ever make.

CHUKAT – *Spies Again*

Towards the end of the *Parsha* Moses sends spies to scout the lands that the nation would need to pass through to get to Israel. Our initial reaction to this is shock. Didn't sending spies lead to the nations wanderings in the wilderness for 40 years? Why would Moses do it again?!

Rashi addresses this question by citing a *Midrash* that explains that the spies convinced Moses that they had total faith in his leadership and in God's promise to give them the land. Seeing their faith, he let them go to spy.

Reflections

There is a saying that "God helps those that help themselves". Although this is usually cited as a knock against faith, there is basis for the statement in Judaism. The Talmud teaches us not to rely on miracles. A person must do everything in his power to work towards a worthy goal. He cannot just sit back and hope for God to grant him his wish. This is the balance. Man must do all he can, while at the same time trusting in God to help him achieve his goals.

PARAH – *Red Mystery*

Many of the laws in the *Torah* seem to have no apparent logic or reason to them. The laws of *Kashrut* are a prime example of this. There is absolutely no logical reason for only eating the meat of animals that have split hooves and that chew their cud. Many of the finest restaurants boast a wide variety of "non-kosher" animals on their menus and they and their customers seem to do quite well. The *Torah* refers to these laws without reasons as *Chukim*, in the plural, and *Chok*, in the singular.

According to the Rabbis, the greatest Chok of all is the Red Heifer, or *Parah Adumah*. When a person comes in contact with a corpse he becomes *Tameh*, or ritually unfit to perform certain holy acts such as entering the Temple, for seven days. In order to become *Tahor*, or ritually fit, he must immerse in a *Mikvah* on the third and seventh days and then have the ashes of a red heifer sprinkled on him by a Kohen. Now, if sprinkling the ashes of a red heifer wasn't strange enough, the Kohen who does the sprinkling becomes *Tameh* himself at the same time that he is making you *Tahor*!

Rabbi Soloveitchik tried to shed some light upon this mysterious ritual as follows. When a person becomes Tameh through any means other than via contact with a corpse he can become *Tahor* simply by immersing himself in a *Mikvah*. No assistance is necessary to achieve the state of *Tahor*. He can accomplish it all by himself. When a person comes into contact with death, however, he cannot become *Tahor* on his own. Death brings to the fore all of the insecurities and fears that we try to hide away in the deepest corners of our mind. It reminds us all that we are just mortals, visitors in the world for only a short time. Faced with this stark reality we are unable to function and are liable to fall into a state of depression. It is in this state of despair that we need the help of others to lead us back to the reality of the living. Therefore, the *Tameh*, through contact with the dead, cannot "cleanse" himself by simply immersing in a *Mikvah*. He needs the assistance of another, the Kohen, to bring him back to his pre-*Tameh* state.

Taking this idea one step further, in order to properly comfort a mourner one needs to feel his sorrow and pain. By so doing, the comforter actually shares in a small part of the *Tumah* of the mourner. Therefore, the Kohen who sprinkles the ashes to purify the *Tameh*, himself becomes *Tameh*, albeit to a lesser degree, since he is only a comforter and not a mourner.

Reflections

The story is told of a family, in a tiny Russian shtetl, whose young son had fallen deathly ill. The doctors gave the boy no chance of recovery. The father decided to travel to Poland to visit a Hasidic Rebbe known for performing miracles. After a long journey by wagon the man arrived in the Polish town and went directly to the Rebbe's house of study where he waited for several hours to see the Rebbe in private. The Rebbe listened compassionately to the man's story and then retired to his private chamber for a half hour. When he emerged the Rebbe told the man that he had left no stone unturned in the heavenly chambers but that there was nothing that he could do to help the man's son. The boy's judgment was sealed.

The man was distraught, but accepted the Rebbe's decision as final, thanked him for his help, and got back on his wagon for the journey home. As he was nearing the town limits the man heard someone screaming for him to stop. He turned around to see the Rebbe running after the wagon. He stopped the wagon and the Rebbe climbed aboard and began apologizing profusely. The man tried to stop him. "Rebbe, I know that you did everything that you could to help my son but it just wasn't part of the heavenly decree. You have nothing to apologize for". The Rebbe answered, "You are right that I could not change the heavenly decree but there is something that I should have done. I should have cried with you, because when a Jew is crying it is the responsibility of every Jew to cry with him."

The Rebbe sat with the man and they both cried from the depths of their souls. At that moment the gates of heaven opened and the decree was torn up. When the man returned home he was greeted by his son, cured and in perfect health.

BALAK –*Impressions*

The *Parsha* of *Balak* deals with the activities of the Moabite king *Balak* and the Gentile prophet Bilaam. Only at the end does it speak about the Jewish People. Why does the *Torah* spend so much time on these non-Jewish characters and events?

The Ishbitzer Rebbe in his commentary "Mey Shiloach" explains that God wanted to show the Jews how the Gentile nations viewed them: with fear and respect. This would give them confidence and self respect.

Reflections

We're often very hard on ourselves. We expect a lot from ourselves and are greatly disappointed if we fail. If we could also see how others view us we would probably be much happier with ourselves. We tend to magnify our own faults and shortcomings to unrealistic levels. When we do something good we often downplay it as something minor and insignificant. Outsiders can see and judge us objectively, applaud our achievements, and accept our failings as normal and forgivable. If we could only see ourselves through the eyes of others....

BALAK – *Basic Instinct*

In this *Parsha* the king of Moab hires the Gentile prophet Bilaam to curse the Jews. As Bilaam rides his donkey, on his way to fulfill his duty, the donkey sees an angel with a drawn sword sent by God to block the way and veers off the road twice. Bilaam, who cannot see the angel, beats the donkey back on to the path on both occasions. Finally the donkey stops completely, unable to pass through a narrow part of the road blocked by the angel. Bilaam, furious, mercilessly beats the donkey. Miraculously, the donkey speaks to Bilaam saying, "What have I done to you that you beat me these three times?" Bilaam replies, "You've embarrassed me. If I had a sword now I would have killed you!" The donkey then replies, "Am I not your donkey that you have been riding for as long as you remember? Have I ever done something like this to you before?" At this point God opens Bilaam's eyes to see the angel standing before him, and Bilaam finally understands God's message to him.

What an amazing story! But since when does God talk to prophets through donkeys? What is the meaning of this story?

The human mind has two parts. The first is the intellectual part that analyzes information methodically and makes rational choices and decisions. With it a person makes decisions based on past experiences, logic, probability, and hard facts.

The second is the instinct. Every person has a basic instinct that I feel is directly connected to that person's soul. That instinct makes decisions based on emotions and feelings that stem from the deepest part of the soul, instead of rational and intellectual analysis and argument. Animals don't have the intellectual part of the mind. All they have is their basic instinct.

Bilaam's intellect told him that it made perfect financial and political sense for him to curse the Jews. Even though his basic instinct, represented by his donkey, knew the right path to follow, his rational mind tried to overpower and suppress it, preventing him from seeing the angel that represented the will of God.

This battle between the intellect (Bilaam) and his basic instinct (donkey) continued until there was nowhere further to go and a permanent and final decision was required. It was then that Bilaam's instinct finally spoke to him and was able to be heard over the noise of his intellect. Once he listened to his basic instinct he was finally able to see the angel and the true path ahead.

Reflections

We all constantly host battles between our intellect and our basic instinct or soul. Although it is important to use our intellect and our rational mind to make decisions, we also need to listen to that instinct and intuition that comes from the deepest part of our soul that sees and knows the right path to take. Both are vital to making the right choices in life. Our basic instinct, that gut feeling we are all familiar with, is usually right. Yet, we often ignore it to follow the path that seems rationally correct. It's important for us to carefully analyze what is really rational and logical for us as opposed to what makes sense for society in general. Sometimes what works for most people is not what's right for us. That's where our instinct comes into play. It usually knows what is truly right for us.

BALAK – *Sneak Attack*

The end of this *Parsha* finds the Jewish People encamped in the mountains of Moab, in the southern part of modern day Jordan near the Dead Sea. After forty years in the wilderness this new generation of Jews is on the doorstep of entering the Promised Land. Then something happens. The *Parsha* tells us that the Jews began worshipping Baal Peor, the idol of the local population, for which they were punished with a plague that killed twenty four thousand of them. How could the Jews fall to the depths of idolatry while so close to the climax of their decades of wandering, the Land of Israel?

A close examination of the verses relating to this episode reveals some possible answers.

At the beginning of the episode the *Torah* says that the Jews "dwelt" in the town of *Shittim*. The term "dwelt" implies a certain degree of permanence or comfort. For the first time in their forty years of solitary travels the Jews set their camp alongside a Gentile people. In this initial experience of integration with the "outside world" the Jews quickly began to assimilate. They were so at ease with and enchanted by this pagan society that they began to throw off the seemingly parochial laws and teachings of the *Torah*.

The *Torah* then tells us that the Jews began to participate in the pagan feasts and idolatrous rituals. The Talmud clarifies that they were enticed into this worship by the Moabite women who seduced them by offering their bodies in exchange for idol worship. The verse then states that the Jews "attached themselves" to the idol Baal Peor. Only then does the verse say that they angered God and were punished. At first the Jews worshiped the idols simply out of their lust for the pagan women, with no idolatrous beliefs or convictions. Had it remained a crime of passion perhaps God would not have punished them so severely. It is only when they "attached themselves" to the idolatry, implying actual belief and sincere worship, did God unleash his wrath upon them.

The road from sanctity to idolatry is usually not short and direct. It usually takes a winding route with sharp curves that hide the road ahead. When the Jews set up camp in *Shittim*, after forty years of total immersion in *Torah*, they undoubtedly had no intention of assimilating into pagan culture. However, human nature is curious and passion is insatiable. In no time large parts of the people were tasting the strange and forbidden waters of paganism. What started off as forbidden passion and lust quickly transformed into real worship.

Reflections

Assimilation is a sly culprit. It sneaks up on us from behind and wears a mask to hide its true identity. When it finally reveals itself it is often too late to fight. The only way to defeat it is to remain firm and vigilant in our practices and beliefs without trying to fit into the forbidden ways of the cultures around us.

BALAK – *Crimes of Passion*

In the midst of the mayhem and confusion precipitated by the seduction of thousands of Jewish men by the women of Moab the *Parsha* recounts how a Jewish man brings a Moabite woman in front of Moses and the entire congregation and cohabits with her, right then and there. In response to this horrifying spectacle Moses and the Jews just stand by and weep as the wrath of God, in the form of a plague, tears through the camp. Finally, Pinchas takes his spear and kills the perpetrators, and the plague ceases. Later on the *Torah* identifies the brazen Jewish perpetrators as the prince of the tribe of Shimon and his companion as a Midianite princess. What is the lesson to be learned from this dramatic episode that warranted it to be highlighted from the general account of idolatry and seduction of the Jewish populace?

The Talmud teaches that the idolatry of the Jews was initially stimulated, not by conviction, but by lust. The Midianite women required the Jews to worship idols in order to live with them. The sins of the Jews were crimes of passion. Their lust overcame their intellect and, in a sense, they could not be held fully responsible for their actions. It was only when they began to become attached to the idols in a religious sense that the wrath of God was kindled against them.

The prince of Shimon, in bringing the woman before the entire congregation, was not acting in the throes of passion. His act was a premeditated attempt to rebel against the laws of the *Torah* and his respected stature, and that of his cohort, made his act all the more brazen. His act of rebellion so shocked and confused the people that all they could do was cry out in despair as the laws of the *Torah* were flouted right in front of their eyes.

The *Torah* is specific in describing how Pinchas took his spear to kill the rebels. The numerical value of the Hebrew word for spear equals 248, which represents the number of prohibitions in the *Torah*. Pinchas used the very laws that they were rebelling against to bring them to justice and show the people that their holy laws would prevail.

There is a difference between sinning from lust or passion and sinning to rebel against the laws of the *Torah*. While the former can conceptually be excused, the latter is inexcusable.

Reflections

It's important to recognize the power of our passions. Only then can we defend against those that are sinful. Ignoring or negating our passions lull us into a state of comfort during which we lower our guard against sin. That's precisely when our "evil inclination" chooses to strike.

Pinchas – *A Covenant of Peace*

In reward for his zealousness in killing the Jewish prince who was publicly engaging in sexual relations with the Midianite princess, God grants Pinchas a "Covenant of Peace". Although the practical details of this covenant are not enumerated, the question is obvious. Why is peace the reward for violence? For example, imagine that you ran the NYC marathon in record-breaking time, against all odds, and after months of arduous training, and as a reward you received a rocking chair. Wouldn't that be absurd? A reward should highlight the achievement and encourage further effort. The message of the rocking chair would be to give up running altogether and "take it easy".

Pinchas committed an appropriate and sanctioned act of violence in defense of his God and people. An appropriate reward for his behavior should have been something that would highlight this zealotry. A "Covenant of Peace" would seem to be a slap in his face implying that his aggression was wrong, yet the *Torah* considers it a reward in the most positive light.

The "Covenant of Peace" was an appropriate reward for Pinchas' zealotry for the following reason. We commonly think of peace as something passive. We view "making peace" as withdrawing from conflict and not taking action. In our personal lives we associate peace with retirement or just "chilling out". Too much thinking implies a lack of peace.

The *Torah*, through Pinchas, teaches us that peace is not passive. Peace needs to be actively and often aggressively pursued. On a national level peace can often be achieved only as a result of strength and vigilance. Egypt signed the Camp David peace treaty with Israel only after failing to destroy Israel on several occasions.

On a personal level we can achieve true peace by actively pursuing our dreams. If we just give up and stay passive we will always feel as though we missed out on opportunities for success and fulfillment. But if we make an effort, even if we don't succeed, we will at least be able to be at peace with ourselves, knowing that we tried our best.

Reflections

Make a list of the things you dream of achieving. What attempts have you made to fulfill these dreams? Just sitting back and hoping that things will happen is usually not the best way to get things done. If you really believe in your dreams then start doing things to make them come true. Then, even if you fail, you will have no regrets because you did everything in your power. You will be at peace with yourself. Of course, you might actually succeed!

May God give us all the strength and desire to pursue our dreams and thereby attain true peace in our lives.

PINCHAS – *A Final Look*

This *Parsha* recounts one of the saddest and most poignant episodes in the entire *Torah*. God tells Moses to go up on one of the mountains of Moab to look over the Jordan River at the land that he will never be allowed to set foot in. Moses climbs the mountain and sees the land that has been his dream to enter for the past forty years and is undoubtedly crushed and heartbroken at his inability to fulfill his greatest desire.

What was so tragic about Moses not being allowed to enter the land? He was the greatest prophet that ever lived and spoke to God "face to face" when receiving the *Torah*. He taught the *Torah* to the Jewish people for eternity and led them out of slavery to freedom. What more could he possibly hope to accomplish that would make him so distraught about not being allowed to enter Israel?

One of the reasons the Land of Israel is called holy is because it provides the Jew with the ability and opportunity to rise to a higher level of holiness and closeness to God. Without the Land of Israel a Jew cannot fulfill his ultimate potential in holiness and spirituality. Moses realized that by not entering Israel, he would never be able to reach this ultimate spiritual height. He knew that the *Torah* of the Diaspora cannot compare to the *Torah* of Israel. He sensed that the food he ate just didn't taste as good or the air he breathed wasn't as sweet as what he could experience in Israel. Despite his greatness and accomplishments he would always be lacking that extra level of holiness that can be attained solely through the Land of Israel. This was his tragedy.

Reflections

For over two thousand years Jews have yearned and sacrificed for the opportunity to set foot in Israel. Most never made it there. We are blessed with the opportunity to travel to Israel in a half day or less. The country has all the luxuries and amenities of the United States and the people are all family. Most importantly, the spiritual benefits of the land are unsurpassed and cannot be duplicated anywhere else.

We have the opportunity to take advantage of the gift that Moses could only dream of by spending as much time as we can, or actually living, in Israel. Let's not pass up this opportunity.

Pinchas - *Taking a Stand*

At the end of the previous *Parsha* Pinchas finds the prince of one of the twelve tribes publicly committing a forbidden sexual act with a Midianite princess and, in a surge of zealotry, kills them. In this week's *Parsha* the name of the prince is mentioned. Why is this necessary?

The Rabbis answer that the *Torah* identified the name of the prince and his position to show the greatness of Pinchas for not being afraid of a powerful man and taking a stand against him. This could not have been an easy thing for Pinchas to do. In our own society we see the practically untouchable status accorded to the wealthy and powerful. No one wants to go up against them for fear of being crushed. Pinchas, however, was so firm in his belief and so clear in the righteousness of his cause that he was able to overcome his fear and awe of the mighty prince to take a stand.

Later in the *Parsha* the *Torah* lists the entire Jewish nation by tribe and family. There are two letters added to each family name, a "*yud*" and a "*hey*". The *Midrash*, cited by Rashi, explains that the "*yud*" and "*hey*" make up the Name of God and were added to the family names in order to dispel the murmurings of the gentile nations claiming that the Jews were really all fathered by their Egyptian slave masters in Egypt. God personally appended His name to testify to the purity of the Jewish nation. God put His Name and reputation at stake to take a stand with His people.

We can all learn such an important lesson from these two episodes. We must always stand up for what we feel is true and right no matter what the odds are against us even if it means putting our own names and reputations at risk. We need to take a stand when the appropriate opportunity presents itself. God did it. Pinchas did it. We too can do it.

MASAI - *End of Story*

Traditionally, the ending of a book contains the main message that the author would like the reader to leave with. The *Torah* can really be divided into two parts. The first four books follow the Jewish People from Creation until the end of their Exodus from Egypt and their arrival to the gates of the Land of Israel. The fifth book, *Devarim*, is called *Mishneh Torah* – the repetition of the *Torah*, because it is just that, a restatement and explanation of the *Torah* by Moses before his death.

Given that the actual story of the Jewish People ends with the conclusion of book four, *Bamidbar*, and the final *Parsha* of that book is *Masai*, it is logical to assume that it contains messages and deals with issues that are of the utmost importance for the reader to leave with and absorb.

The *Parsha* of *Masai* primarily deals with two issues: settling the Land of Israel and designating cities of refuge. The importance of conquering and settling the Land of Israel is clear, despite a disagreement among the biblical commentators as to the exact character of the *Mitzvah*. Without possession of the land a large portion of the commandments, including all agricultural and Temple related laws, cannot be fulfilled. In addition, many of the *Mitzvot* that are able to be fulfilled in the Diaspora cannot be applied to their fullest potential. Although *Shabbat*, *Kashrut*, Holidays, and issues of personal status certainly apply in the Diaspora, only in a Jewish controlled Israel can they be applied on a national scale and to national institutions such as the army and the government.

Most importantly, however, is the idea that all *Mitzvot* performed in the Land of Israel have greater spiritual significance because of the unique status and holiness of the land itself. The Talmud even goes so far as to remark that "the very air of the Land of Israel perpetuates wisdom" and that "there is no *Torah* like the *Torah* of Israel". The *Mitzvah* of possessing the Land of Israel is, therefore, highlighted at the end of the Book of *Bamidbar*.

The laws of the Cities of Refuge are also found at the end of *Bamidbar*. What is their grand significance that warrants their position at the end of the book? The purpose of the cities of refuge were to provide sanctuary for someone who killed another purely as a result of negligence, with absolutely no premeditation or intention to harm. Banishment to the city of refuge is referred to in the Talmud as *Galut* or Exile. Although the term usually refers to banishment outside of the borders of Israel, by using it within the borders the Talmud is teaching us an important lesson. Even someone living in the Land of Israel can be alienated from his heritage and people or, in other words, in exile. Simply living in the land is not enough.   However, *Torah* study and observance combined with the Land of Israel can raise a Jew to the highest levels of holiness and spirituality.

Masay — *Journeys*

The *Torah* lists the forty two journeys that the Jews traveled from their departure from Egypt until their entrance into the Land of Israel. The obvious question is as follows. Since the *Torah* is a guide for eternity, what is the purpose of including a list of journeys taken during the forty years of wandering in the wilderness?

Rashi cites two approaches to answer this question. The first explains that the *Torah* listed all of the journeys to show that God was merciful and didn't make the Jews wander too much. The first twelve journeys occurred during the first year after the Exodus and the last eight were taken in the final year of wandering. Therefore, out of the total of forty two only twenty journeys were made during the remaining thirty eight years in the wilderness. One journey every two years doesn't seem that bad.

The second approach explains the reason for the list of journeys as a way of telling the Jews to remember their trials and tribulations, to learn and grow from them. The parable offered to illustrate this point is of a father who carries his sick son from their home to the doctor in a far off town. On their trip back home, after the son is cured, the father reminds the son of the hardships endured on each stop of the journey.

These two approaches explaining the journeys of the wilderness can also be used to deal with our own personal journeys. For example, how do we deal with a year long relationship that fails? The first approach is to minimize. It's not so bad. It was only one year of my entire life. I'm not going to let that one period of time stop me from enjoying the rest of my life. The second approach is to revisit, review, and analyze the relationship and the things that we did right and wrong in order to learn and grow from it. Both of these approaches are necessary, each in its proper measure.

The Book

Of

Devarim

"Restatement"

DEVARIM – *Partners With God*

The *Parsha* of *Devarim* begins the Book of *Devarim*, or Deuteronomy, the fifth of the Five Books of Moses. This fifth book is also called *Mishneh Torah*, the repetition of the *Torah*, because it consists of Moses restating and explaining portions of the *Torah* to the Jewish People.

After describing the geographical setting, the *Parsha* states, "Moses began to explain the *Torah*, saying." The rest of the *Parsha*, and the entire Book, is the content of his explanation. It is also Moses' final message to the people before they enter the Promised Land. As such, it would seem logical for Moses to encourage the people for their upcoming battles to conquer the land. Towards the end of the *Parsha* Moses does this by reminding the people of their victories against the kings Sihon and Og. At the beginning of his "explanation", however, Moses reminds the Jews of two events that come across as anything but encouraging. First Moses recounts how he was forced to set up a court system due to the overwhelming litigiousness of the people. Then he recounts the incident of the spies. Why does Moses start out his explanation of the *Torah*, and his final "pep talk" to the people, with these two negative events?

Actually, there is a much greater question regarding the entire Book of *Devarim*. The *Torah* is very careful to use no extra words, or even letters, yet it includes an entire book that basically repeats the laws and events already recorded. Why was it necessary for Moses to "explain" the *Torah*?

God wants man to be a partner in His laws and teachings. The *Torah* was given in such a way as to allow man the opportunity to use his mind to uncover the meanings, details, and secrets of its teachings. The Oral *Torah*, which today is embodied primarily in the Talmud, contains the divinely ordained methods for deriving, explaining, and interpreting the word of God. When man studies the Talmud he is entering into and engaging in a partnership with God.

The Book of *Devarim*, through the example of Moses "explaining" the *Torah*, teaches us this lesson. The incidents of the judges and the spies recounted by Moses at the beginning of his address reinforce this lesson.

The idea to establish a court system came from Yitro, Moses' non Jewish father in law. Although God approved it, the creativity and initiative stemmed from the human mind. The court system is a prime example of Man's partnership with God. Although the incident of the spies turned into a tragic mistake that cost the Jews forty years of wandering in the desert, nevertheless, it was a product of human initiative. By recounting the spy incident Moses is teaching us that, with the proper intentions, making mistakes is part of the process of explaining and interpreting *Torah*.

True *Torah* study involves questioning, searching for truth, and using every bit of our God given intellect to properly understand the will of God. This is the secret of being partners with God.

EIKEV – *In the Hands of Heaven*

In this *Parsha* Moses rhetorically asks the Jewish People, "What does God ask of you?" He continues by answering that all God wants is for you to love and fear him and to observe all the commandments. Is that all? Isn't that a tall order to expect from the people?

Rashi cites the *Midrash* that derives from these verses that everything is in the hands of heaven except for fear of heaven. What does fear of heaven really mean? I think it means complete faith. Based on this explanation we can better understand Moses' question and answer. The only thing that God demands of us is for us to have faith in Him. Man strives to gain control over every aspect of life, but usually realizes that it is an impossible task.

The following story illustrates this point. A wealthy ship owner had lost all contact with one of his ships at sea for several weeks and had no way of finding out its location or condition. He went to visit a famous fortuneteller who could see into the unknown through her crystal ball, with the hope of finding where his ship was. The fortuneteller peered into her crystal ball. "I see a terrible storm battering your ship in the Mediterranean Sea. It doesn't look like the ship will make it through the storm." The merchant was devastated since his entire fortune was being transported on that very ship. He quickly began praying as he had never prayed before. Suddenly the fortune teller exclaimed, "Wait! I see something. The storm has stopped. Your prayers really must have helped." Without giving the merchant much of a chance to rejoice, the fortuneteller continued, "I see that there is a shipment of illegal contraband on the ship. If the ship safely docks in port the authorities will find the contraband and arrest you, as the owner of the ship." Once again the merchant began fervent prayers to bring the storm back. The fortuneteller then remarked that the storm had indeed returned, but that she now saw one new piece of information. "I see that your only son is on the ship". Now, the merchant began praying for the storm to cease. Soon after, the fortuneteller informed him that the storm had indeed stopped but that the island that the ship was heading towards was filled with ferocious cannibals who would not only kill, but also devour his son.

The merchant could stand it no longer and, throwing up his hands, cried out, "God, I don't know what to pray for anymore because I don't know what is really good for me, so please, just do whatever the right thing for me is."

We're not expected to control the course of events in our lives. Only super heroes in the comics can do that. God doesn't want us to be super heroes. What He does want is to see us live our lives with faith. That doesn't mean that we don't need to try to influence our environment and the events that affect us. It does mean that we also need to take a step back to examine what God is putting before us and to decide if it is something worth embracing. For example, so many of us are so sure we know what our perfect mate is supposed to be like that we are quick to reject wonderful people that are thrown right before our faces. We know what is best for us and we control our destinies. How many of us stop to think that perhaps God is sending these people to us because they are really good for us? How many of us have the faith to put aside our self conceived notions and actually give these people a chance?

God doesn't want us to give up all control over our lives. All He wants is for us to have a little faith that He is actually watching over us and leading us in the direction that is right for us. All we can do is to have faith. The rest is in the "hands of heaven".

RE'EH – *Slavery or Freedom*

In this *Parsha* Moses reviews the laws relating to the treatment of servants. The *Torah* teaches that a Jewish indentured servant may only serve for a maximum period of six years. If at the end of the six years, however, he or she decides to remain in servitude, the master must pierce the servant's ear with a nail against a doorpost, adjacent to the mezuzah. The servant must then spend either the rest of his life, or until the Jubilee year, in servitude. The reason given by the Talmud for the ear piercing is that, the same ear that heard God free the Jews from slavery and give them the laws of the *Torah* is now choosing to be a slave to a new master.

Although actual indentured servitude and slavery have long since been eradicated in the civilized world, the lesson of this *Torah* law is possibly more relevant today than ever. The Talmud teaches that a free man is one who is bound by the *Torah*. The laws of the *Torah*, including the restrictions, actually free man from being a slave to the whims of society. They force man to be different. They create individualists rather than followers.

Abraham, the father of Judaism, was called "Ivri" meaning, "from the other side". The simple explanation of this is that Abraham came from the other side of the Euphrates River in Mesopotamia. The Talmud teaches that the entire world was on one side and Abraham was on the other side. The entire world worshiped idols. How easy would it have been for Abraham to just join in and "go with the flow"? Instead Abraham chose to follow his belief in God and be free.

The laws of *Shabbat* are another unlikely example of freedom. The *Shabbat* is supposed to be a day of connecting with our spirituality and of bonding with family and community. To accomplish these goals we break away from the everyday tasks that monopolize our time and energy. A person who is unable to shut off a cell phone or TV for a day is a slave to it. A person who can't take a day off from work is also a slave, no matter how much money he earns or how high a position she attains. Observing the *Shabbat*, with all of the *Torah*'s restrictions, is a sign of freedom.

Why would any servant willingly subject himself to voluntary servitude rather than going free, as in the *Torah's* case of the ear piercing? Unfortunately, we see the answer all around us, possibly even in our own lives. How many of us have voluntarily enslaved ourselves to work, money, fashion, and the society around us? Fortunately, we have the key to freedom: the *Torah*. All we need to do is look within it to be free. The choice is yours, slavery or freedom.

SHOFTIM – *Thinking and Doing*

It is no coincidence that the *Parsha* of *Shoftim* always coincides with the week of *Rosh Chodesh Elul*, the beginning of the High Holiday season. In *Shoftim* the *Torah* commands us to appoint judges and law enforcement officers. Why does the *Torah* require a separation of duties? Why can't the judges also enforce the laws?

The skill set and thought process for judgment and enforcement are totally different, requiring different individuals to perform each role. A judge must carefully weigh and consider all arguments and possibilities in a case. In criminal cases he must also, according to *Torah* law, pursue even the slightest opportunity of finding the defendant innocent of the crimes charged.

A law enforcement officer is not permitted to consider the validity of the judgment. His job is not to analyze the merits of the case or evaluate the characters of the plaintiff and defendant. His job is solely to carry out the sentence imposed by the judge's verdict.

Each person must apply the commandment to appoint judges and enforcers to his own life. A person's judge must make life decisions based on an analysis of facts, personal experience, and gut instinct. We all try to convince ourselves to do things that we probably shouldn't by imagining all the rewards if we did. The *Torah* warns us that bribery will sway the judge's heart and prevent him from making a correct decision. So too may an individual not bribe himself into making a decision.

Once a person makes the "right" decision he must carry it out. This is the hard part for it is one thing to decide to do something and plan it all out. It's quite another to actually do it. This is where the enforcer comes in. Without the enforcer all the thinking, planning and committing is worthless. The enforcer in each person carries out the verdict. The judge and the enforcer can't exist independently of the other.

SHOFTIM — *Seeing the Future*

The *Torah* warns us not to rely on fortune tellers and diviners to determine the future. Instead, the *Torah* tells us to rely on God with complete innocence and faith. Rashi explains that we should take whatever happens to us as part of God's plan, and not try to plan our actions according to some system of discerning the future.

A popular method of "divination" is astrology, which claims that a person's entire life is predestined, and evaluates a person's future based on the position of the cosmos at the time of the person's birth. The Talmud teaches that God told Abraham that the Jewish People will not be ruled by astrology. A Jew's astrological chart it will have absolutely no bearing on his future as long as he follows the *Torah,* which is above and beyond the control of the cosmos. *Torah* takes destiny out of the hands of the astrologers and soothsayers and places it into the hands of every Jew willing to accept it.

Events sometimes occur that appear to be signs from heaven. These signs seem to indicate to us what to do and what direction to take. The only problem with these signs is that they can often be interpreted in many ways, both positive and negative. Trying to interpret them usually leaves us just as confused as before.

This is exactly what the *Torah* is referring to when it tells us to rely on God with complete faith (*Tmimim*). The *Torah* is the action plan for every Jew. By following the *Torah* we can be completely positive that we are going in the right direction. Signs can be nice motivators, but our actions can only be guided by the *Torah*. Then we can be sure that we have chosen correctly.

KI TEYTZEY - *Changes*

This *Parsha* begins with the verse, "When you will go out to war against your enemy, and God will give them to you in victory and you will take prisoners". The *Torah* goes on to describe a very unusual law. If, while in battle, a Jewish soldier captures a woman that he desires he may take her as a wife as long as she leaves behind her idolatrous beliefs and converts to Judaism. Before being allowed to marry this captive the soldier must allow her to mourn her parents by allowing her to shave her head, wear sackcloth, and generally neglect her appearance for a period of thirty days. Only then, if he stills desires her, does the *Torah* permit them to wed.

Looking beyond the literal and technical aspects of this law the Chassidic Masters explain that going out to war refers to every person's battle against their own evil inclination. When, with God help, we are successful in our battle we often face difficult issues regarding our past actions. When a person becomes more observant they often must make changes to the way they conduct their lives and their relationships. But what about the good things in their "past life"? For example, a dancer might feel that she must give up her dancing in order to lead a *Torah* life or a comedian might think he needs to give up jokes to be "religious".

The message of this *Parsha* is that if in our personal victorious war (*teshuvah*) we take a captive that we find beautiful (the good things in our past) we need not dispose of it. Rather we can try to integrate it into our new lifestyle. We might have to make some minor adaptations but we can certainly continue to enjoy our beloved "captive" within the context of a *Torah* lifestyle. Talents, culture, humor, sports and entertainment can all be successfully integrated into *Torah* living. May we all merit to be victorious in our personal wars and to make the right life changes and decisions in a healthy and beneficial way.

KI TAVO – *Without Fanfare*

This *Parsha* begins by describing the ceremony of *Bikurim*, the presenting of the first fruits to the Kohen in Jerusalem. The farmer presents his basket of produce to the Kohen and then recites an uplifting abridged summary of Jewish history beginning with Jacob's sojourn in Egypt, through the slavery and exodus, and culminating with the settlement of Israel. The entire ceremony is joyous and uplifting.

The *Parsha* then describes the tithing ceremony whereby the farmer separates one tenth of his crop, in the third year of the seven year cycle, and gives it to the Levites and the needy. Unlike in the *Bikurim* ceremony, the farmer recites a confession when giving the tithe. In this confession the farmer affirms that he did not transgress any of the tithing regulations mandated by the *Torah* and that he followed the word of God completely. Based on this confession the farmer asks God to watch over and bless the Jewish People and the land of Israel.

Why does the *Bikurim* ceremony have such a festive mood and the tithing ceremony such an introspective and serious one?

When it comes to donating either money or time to a new, high profile cause people get excited. The *Bikurim* ceremony was such an opportunity. All the farmers would take their best and newest produce up to the holy city of Jerusalem where they would mingle and showoff their produce with all the other farmers before presenting their offering to a distinguished Kohen in the holy Temple. It was an exciting event filled with honor and pageantry, celebrated by the entire nation.

On the other hand, the tithing ceremony was done in private in the middle of the seven year cycle. The produce was not taken up to Jerusalem to be given to the Kohen in the Holy Temple. Rather it was given to the Levites or to the simple paupers wherever the farmer lived. There was no pageantry, celebrations, or public displays attached to the tithing. There were no plaques, medals, or dinners honoring the donors. Because of this the farmer didn't have the same motivation to give as with *Bikurim*. It was feared that perhaps the farmer would shirk his responsibility and try to pass unnoticed. Therefore the *Torah* commanded the farmer to recite a confession affirming that he performed his duty properly. Once the farmer confesses it becomes clear that his intentions were pure and that he gave his tithe not for public honor but for the *Mitzvah* of helping others. In reward for this God watches over and blesses the Jewish People and the land of Israel.

Reflections

Everyone loves giving to high profile causes where their contribution will be honored and publicized. Most people are not so excited when it comes to the mundane but necessary projects that need support. We should all try to support worthy causes even though they might not lead to public notice or honor. If we do God will surely look favorably upon us and grant us success and happiness.

NITZAVIM – *Only for the Children*

This *Parsha* tells us that the entire people of Israel gathered to accept the covenant of God's *Torah*. The *Torah* specifically includes the children in this gathering. How can children enter into a binding contract? What can we learn from the children?

During an Israel trip, the group I lead visited sick children at Hadassah hospital in Jerusalem. After I played guitar and lead our group in singing for the children we came to cheer up, I was asked, by the hospital administrator, if I would visit a boy with a serious genetic disorder who loved music. I went to the boy's bedside and played some songs in honor of his upcoming *Bar-Mitzvah*. He was overjoyed. I then asked him if he had a favorite song that he would like to hear. He proceeded to sing, in a very sweet and beautiful voice, a popular Jewish song whose lyrics (when translated) are, "we are believers, the children of believers, and the only one we can rely on is God. The people of Israel trust in God, He is their shield and savior". Just thinking of this brings tears to my eyes -- tears of pride. Even in all of his pain this young Jewish boy, soon to become a *Bar-Mitzvah*, was able to express the essence of our people and of our faith. He is a Jewish hero.

Children are blessed with the ability to see truth in the world. While adults view things in the context of their own visions and desires children see things the way they really are. No rationalizations or interpretations. The truth, and nothing but the truth. This is why the children were commanded to accept the covenant along with their parents, for only the children could truly testify to the truth of the *Torah* and to accept it with no ulterior motives or conditions.

May we all be blessed with the courage and purity of that little boy in Hadassah hospital and with the eyes of children, to see the truth in our lives and in the world.

Festivals

and

Holy Days

ELUL – *Getting Ready*

A Chassidic story: A wealthy merchant would regularly visit the Baal Shem Tov and donate large sums of money for the Rebbe's charitable causes. Eventually his fortune changed and his business failed, leaving him nearly penniless. When he went to visit the Rebbe again the Baal Shem, undoubtedly aware of the man's dire straits, asked him for a huge donation of 400 rubles to aid the victims of an earthquake in the holy city of Tzvat. The man left upset and angry. How could the Rebbe be so insensitive as to request such a huge sum from him, knowing of his financial hardships? The man returned home and told his wife what happened. He then went out to think of a plan for how to raise the funds. While he was gone his wife gathered all the silver utensils in the house and went to the market to sell them. She brought back the coins and spent the entire evening polishing them. When the man returned home his wife presented him with a bag of coins. The next morning the man brought the coins to the Rebbe. When the Baal Shem emptied the coins onto the table he was taken aback by their shining brilliance. He blessed the man and asked how the coins had gotten so shiny. The man had no answer. When the man returned he told his wife what had happened at the Rebbe's and asked her where she had found such shiny coins. The wife answered that the coins weren't shiny when she got them. However, since she knew that they would be in the presence of the Rebbe she stayed up for hours polishing them until they sparkled.

Reflections

In a few weeks we will all stand in the presence of "Our Father, Our King". Although we might be a bit dirty, we should take this opportunity to polish ourselves up so that we can shine before Him. Let's pick one or two things we feel we can "polish" in ourselves, and work on them. Even if we feel we won't be able to keep it up for the long term, at least we'll shine for the High Holy Days. It's not hypocritical: it's just taking one small step at a time, and being the best we can be right now.

Rosh Hashanah – *A Time to Cry?*

In addition to being the beginning of the new year and the anniversary of the creation of Man, the holiday of Rosh Hashanah is also known as the Day of Judgment. The Day of Judgment evokes feelings of fear and repentance, which are reflected in the Selichot, the supplications for forgiveness that are said on the days before and after the holiday. Why, then, are no Selichot said on the actual holiday of Rosh Hashanah? If it is a Day of Judgment, wouldn't it make sense to beg for forgiveness on it?

Although no actual prayers for forgiveness are offered, we do offer perhaps the most powerful supplication: the Shofar. The *Midrash* teaches that the sounds of the shofar represent the sounds of crying. The form of these sounds is derived from the cries of the mother of an infamous pagan general, Sisera, killed by the Jews in the times of the Judges. When we blow the shofar we are crying out to God for forgiveness and mercy.

Why was a gentile women used as the paradigm for crying out? Whereas the cries of a Jew are imbued with intrinsic spirituality and holiness, the cries of a gentile are generated from the depths of the most basic and simplest part of the soul. The cry of the shofar is meant to represent that simplest and most basic form of prayer.

We do not sound the shofar on *Shabbat*. The reason given in the Talmud is to prevent someone from violating the *Shabbat* by carrying a shofar in the public domain. There is, I think, a deeper reason too. *Shabbat* represents the perfection of the completion of creation. *Shabbat* does not lack anything. It is complete – Shalem. Crying out implies lacking. Since we do not lack anything on *Shabbat* we cannot cry out through the Shofar.

Reflections

The sounds of the shofar act as the prayer of those Jews who don't know how to pray with words. When a person cries out, no words are necessary.

ROSH HASHANA - *Just Dance*

It was told that in the shul of the great Chassidic Master, the Chozeh (Seer) of Lublin, they sang and danced on the night of Rosh Hashanah. When the Misnagdim, the anti-Chassidic proponents, heard of this they were taken aback. How could the renown Rebbe allow dancing on the awesome Day of Judgment? They decided to send a spy to the Chozeh's synagogue to investigate.

The undercover Misnaged traveled to Lublin on the eve of the new year and witnessed the community diligently preparing for the holy day. That night, in the synagogue of the Chozeh, the mood was serious while the Chassidim fervently prayed for a favorable heavenly judgment. Everything seemed very proper until the services ended. Then the Chassidim moved the benches to the side and began joyously singing and dancing with all their might. The Misnaged, unable to contain his anger, ran up to the Chozeh and reprimanded him. "How can you allow this merriment on the Day of Judgment?" Without replying the Chozeh placed his hand over the man's eyes allowing him to see a vision. In the vision the man saw the gates of the Garden of Eden within which a group of Jews danced fervently in a circle. Outside of the gates stood one man, watching and crying, unable to enter. The Chozeh removed his hand and the Misnaged realized that he was the solitary man in the vision prevented from entering the Garden of Eden. He began to cry and plead with the Chozeh. "Rebbe, how can I too dance with the men in the Garden of Eden?" The Chozeh replied, "Just dance".

Reflections

So many times we think about doing something, but never end up doing it because we feel it is something that is, perhaps, good for others, but not something that we could ever do. We see others singing and praying and we wish we could have the same spirit and fervor. We see others doing *Mitzvot* and we wonder how it would feel if we did them as well. We think, "how good would it be if we could attend prayer services every *Shabbat*."

The Chozeh of Lublin gave us the secret of success and fulfillment. If you want to join the Jews that are dancing in the Garden of Eden, just join them and dance. Just sing and pray and do *mitzvot* and go to shul. Don't just think about it. Try it. Do it. See how it feels for you.

On Rosh Hashanah we pray to God for health and peace, the things we have no control over. For everything else we need to make the effort to have a sweet year. Much of it is in our hands. If we want to have a great year of growth and success, make it happen. Just dance.

YOM KIPPUR - *Take Two*

The days between Rosh Hashanah and Yom Kippur are called the *Aseret Yi-May Teshuvah* – Ten Days of Repentance, and the *Shabbat* that falls during those days is called *Shabbat Shuva* (Return). According to our tradition God is especially receptive to our prayers and pleas during these days.

Rabbi Pinchas Teitz Z"L, a great Rabbi and Scholar who was the founder and dean of the Yeshiva in Elizabeth, NJ that I attended for elementary and high school, used to address the student body of the Yeshiva every year during these Days of Repentance. Every year he repeated the same parable that touched my heart in its simplicity and depth, and has stayed with me since.

Imagine taking a final exam that will decide your entire academic career. You've studied for the test, but as you take it you become so nervous that you forget all the material. You struggle through the exam and, with a heavy heart, you hand in your exam booklet with the almost certain knowledge that you got many of the answers wrong. You feel like a failure. Suddenly your entire class is called back into the exam room. The teacher makes an incredible announcement. Every student can take back his or her exam and change any answers that they think are wrong before returning it for grading. Can you even imagine that?! A second chance! A dream come true.

This is the essence of the Days of Repentance. Our judgment has been inscribed on Rosh Hashanah. We leave court dejected and afraid. Surely, judging by our actions of the past year, we have not merited a favorable verdict. All is lost. But then God calls us back and gives us our personal verdict book, and the amazing opportunity to change its contents. We have the ability, during these ten days, to rewrite our verdict before it is sealed on Yom Kippur. What a wondrous gift.

Let us all take this special gift and use these days to make changes in ourselves and in our relationships with others. If we make a sincere effort right now, we can be sure that the verdict that is sealed on Yom Kippur will be the right one for us.

YOM KIPPUR – *Approaching God*

One of the greatest gifts given to the Jewish People by God is the ability to repent – Teshuvah. Part of the Teshuvah process is crying out to God in supplication and repentance. How does one cry out to God?

The traditional form of communication with God is through prayer. The Sages composed the traditional prayer service, and hid within its words the secret formulas to unlock the mysteries of the heavens and the gates of atonement. In fact, the *Torah* in Genesis teaches that God created the world with the words, "Let there be light." The Kabbalists derive from this that the letters of the Hebrew alphabet possess the power of creation. Therefore, for those who are capable, it is highly efficacious to pray in the original Hebrew syntax.

For those who cannot pray in Hebrew, the Talmud clearly teaches that the prayers can be recited in any language understood by the petitioner. What if the words of the prayer book simply do not stir the heart of the supplicant? Then he should use his own words to cry out to God from the depths of his emotions.

However, what if the person standing before the Creator is so broken with pain and sorrow that he cannot even utter a single word in prayer? What if no sound comes forth from his throat, as hard as he might try to scream out?

King David, in the Psalms, says, "I am a prayer." What does this mean? For example, when you encounter a homeless beggar on the street with his hand outstretched, palm facing up, he doesn't need to deliver a fundraising pitch to let you know that he is in desperate need. All you need to do is to take one look at him to know he needs your help. His whole presence screams out to you. This is exactly what King David is saying. His whole physical being was transformed into a supplication, without him uttering a single word.

On Rosh Hashanah the sounding of the shofar is our deepest and most powerful prayer because it transcends words, and emanates from the depths of every Jewish soul regardless of its linguistic or oratorical skill level. The same is true when we join together in a *Niggun*, which is a song with no words.

On Yom Kippur our fasting transforms our bodies into humble vessels of supplication. Therefore, when we come before God on Yom Kippur with broken hearts and shattered egos, humbly bowed before Him with outstretched hands like simple beggars, we ourselves become prayers. Our very presence cries out to God for health, love, success, peace and salvation. No words are necessary.

May God bless us all with the strength to be able to cry out to Him in whatever way we are best able to, and may He answer all of our prayers and seal us all in the Book of Life.

Succot - *With Complete Faith*

The Talmud states two reasons for the *Mitzvah* of living in the Succah for seven days. The first is to commemorate that our ancestors dwelled in Succahs in the wilderness. The second is to remember the "clouds of glory" that surrounded and protected the Jews in the desert. The Talmud seems to lean towards the second explanation. If this is correct, why do we use a hut to represent the clouds? Wouldn't it make more sense for us to live out in the open air, under the clouds? Wouldn't that give us more of a feeling of complete dependence on the protection given us by God?

Although, in truth, living out "under the clouds" starkly represents total dependence on God, real life isn't as clear cut. We all try to build structures to provide us with security and protection. We live in these structures and feel safe and in control. We view these structures as permanent, and without them we cannot function. The reality, however, is that our structures are really just flimsy huts that create for us the illusion of permanence and security. They fall apart when we least expect them too.

The Succah that we live in for seven days reminds us that our own structures of security − our houses, careers, social status − are just temporary. They last for a week, a month, a year, several years, but are then taken down. The Succah reminds us that our real security and protection comes not from the walls that we build but from the graces of God.

May we all be blessed with the wisdom to differentiate between the security that is true and comes only from God, and the false security of the hut that looks real, but is only an illusion.

The Simcha of Succot

Every Jewish holiday has a main theme that is illustrated and defined by the *Mitzvot* and activities associated with it. The main theme of Pesach is freedom, which is illustrated by the Seder, Matzah, wine, and reclining. The main theme of *Shavuot* is *Torah* study and therefore, we stay up all night studying. Rosh Hashanah, the Day of Judgment, is represented by the shofar sounds that wake us up to repentance and Yom Kippur, the Day of Atonement, is defined by fasting, confession and repentance.

What is the main theme of *Succot* and how is that theme illustrated by the *Mitzvot* of *Succot*? Tradition teaches that the main theme of Succot is *Simcha*, happiness. According to the *Torah* each of the Festivals contains an obligation of *Simcha*. How is *Simcha* unique to *Succot* and how do the *Mitzvot* of *Succot* illustrate *Simcha*?

Mitzvot can be categorized into several types:
- *Mitzvot* that revolve around an object. For example, the *lulav*, *shofar* and *tefilllin*.
- *Mitzvot* that depend on a person's actions. For example, blessings, *Torah* study, *Chesed*, and prayer.
- *Mitzvot* that depend on time. For example, *Shabbat* and Festivals. Making Kiddush over wine on Thursday is meaningless. That same action on Friday night is a *Mitzvah*.
- *Mitzvot* that depend on a specific geographic location. There are *mitzvot* that only apply within the borders of the land of Israel, of Jerusalem, and of the Temple. Another example is *Shushan Purim*, which only applies to cities that were walled in the time of Joshua.

I would like to suggest a fifth category: space. Every action that is done within a defined space is considered to be a *Mitzvah*. There are two examples of the space category.

The first is divinely mandated. According to the Talmud any action performed in the land of Israel is considered a *Mitzvah*. For example, the Talmud says that even walking four cubits in Israel is a *Mitzvah*.

The second is manmade. The Succah is a space we create within which every act we perform is automatically defined as serving God. Reading a book, eating, sleeping, schmoozing and singing are all examples of seemingly mundane activities that are transformed into "*Mitzvot*" when performed in a Succah.

What is the definition of *Simcha*? The Talmud defines *Simcha* as the consumption of meat and wine. This is why it is customary to eat meat and drink wine on the festivals. When commanding us to be happy on the festivals the verse in the *Torah* says, "*Vihayita Ach Sameach*" meaning "and you should be completely happy". Since the *Torah* already commanded us to be happy, why does the *Torah* need to repeat this message again by telling us to be "completely happy?" In any case, how can a person be "completely happy?" There are inevitably things in life that don't make us happy or, at the very least, are neutral.

To answer this question I'd like to suggest a different definition of Simcha. Unhappiness often stems from conflict. The conflict can be external or internal. We are constantly questioning and judging our motives and actions and trying to choose the right path to take. Sometimes everything we do becomes the subject of an internal conflict and we never can experience the peace of mind we crave. True happiness is, in fact, peace of mind. We are happy when we have no conflicts to deal with and we can just relax and be at peace. When we are totally focused on a single objective and all of our actions are geared towards a specific goal and ideal that we believe in, we remove uncertainty and conflict and become "complete" or "*shalem.*" *Shlaymut,* completeness, is equal to peace of mind and happiness.

The Succah represents *Shlaymut* since everything we do in the Succah, even the most mundane activity, is channeled towards the single goal of holiness. The *Simcha* of the festival of *Succot* is *Shlaymut,* which is illustrated by the Succah.

The ultimate next step is to make the entire universe our Succah within which all of our actions can be channeled towards holiness. The holiday of *Shmini Atzeret*, which has no *Mitzvot* other than pure *Simcha*, represents this metaphysical Succah. This idea is also expressed in our prayer for God to spread his Succah of peace over the entire world.

We so often separate our spiritual lives from our worldly ones. This often creates conflict and unhappiness. All we need to do is create that space, build that Succah, to achieve a sense of purpose, fulfillment, *Shlaymut*, and happiness.

Simchat Torah – *Hakafot*

It is the custom to carry the *Torah* around the synagogue seven times on *Simchat Torah*. These circuits are called *Hakafot*. According to Rabbi J.B. Soloveitchik, God is symbolically in the center of the circle, or *Hakafot*, we make with the *Torah*.

The Talmud, at the end of the tractate *Taanit,* teaches that at the end of days the righteous will form a circle in the Garden of Eden and God will stand in the center. The righteous will all point towards God and proclaim, "This is our God whom we have trusted in and who saved us. This is God whom we have trusted in, we will rejoice in his salvation." What is the significance of the circle in both the *Hakafot* and the story in the Talmud?

The Talmud teaches that there are seventy faces to the *Torah*. That means that although there is a set and accepted standard of *Torah* observance and interpretation, beyond that point there are many valid ways of interpreting and following the words of the *Torah*. In the first blessing of the Amidah we say, "The God of Abraham, God of Isaac, and God of Jacob." Why not just say, the God of Abraham, Isaac, and Jacob"? The Shlah Hakadosh answers that it is to teach us that each of the Patriarchs had a unique relationship with the Almighty. So too every Jew develops a unique and personal relationship with God which is unlike any other.

The geometric uniqueness of a circle is that every point along its lines is exactly equidistant from its center point. As long as the *Torah* is at the center of our circle it doesn't matter exactly where along that circle we personally place ourselves. Everyone finds their own location within the boundaries of the circle of *Torah* and creates their own relationship with God, which is no closer or no farther than anyone else's relationship.

This idea is reinforced by the story in the Talmud, where the righteous form a circle and all point to God. It doesn't matter where they fall on the circle. As long as they are a part of that circle they can all equally point to God and proclaim his greatness.

SIMCHAT TORAH — *Why Now?*

The holiday of *Simchat Torah* celebrates the annual completion of the reading of the *Torah* and the start of a new *Torah* reading cycle. The holiday is celebrated on *Shmini Atzeret* in Israel and on the day after in the Diaspora. Since *Shavuot* is the holiday that celebrates the giving of the *Torah* on Sinai it would seem to make more sense to celebrate *Simchat Torah* on *Shavuot*. Why, then, do we begin and end the *Torah* reading cycle on, or right after, *Shmini Atzeret*?

The story is told of a man imprisoned for life, who is offered his freedom if he will marry the king's daughter. The man is torn. On the one hand, this is his only chance for freedom. On the other hand, if the king is offering his daughter to a prisoner, she must be extremely hideous in every way. After thinking over his options the man chooses freedom and reluctantly resigns himself to marrying the king's daughter. When the wedding day finally arrives the man enters under the chupah with a feeling of despair and defeat. He experiences no happiness on his wedding day. However, after spending his first year of freedom with his new wife the man finally begins to see the good and beauty in her. To celebrate his newfound happiness the man decides to throw a huge a party.

The Jews were freed from their bondage in Egypt on the condition that they would receive the *Torah* on Sinai. They probably assumed that if God was offering this *Torah* to a group of slaves, it must not be something of great value to rejoice about. Only after spending time getting acquainted with the *Torah* by studying it could they truly appreciate its greatness and rejoice over it. This appreciation was realized on *Shmini Atzeret*.

There is another reason, I think, why *Simchat Torah* occurs on *Shmini Atzeret*. The *Midrash* teaches that one of the reasons for the holiday of *Shmini Atzeret*, which has no special *Mitzvot* associated with it, is that God tells the Jewish People that "it is difficult for Me to have you separate from Me, so I will prolong the holiday season with an extra holiday, *Shmini Atzeret*."

God gives us the opportunity to draw close to Him through the study of *Torah* and performance of *Mitzvot*. During the High Holiday season we immerse ourselves in these activities and, thereby, draw closer to God. However, once Succot is over we return back to what is commonly referred to as "reality". By doing so, we separate ourselves from God. The holiday of *Simchat Torah* reminds us that by engaging in the study of *Torah* we can stay close to God. We don't have to separate and say goodbye once the holiday season is over. We can maintain that same closeness to God year round. All we need to do is study *Torah*.

CHANUKAH – *Fire or Light*

(Based on the writings of Rav Shlomo Y. Zevin)

There are two ways to view the kindling of the *Menorah*: the creation of fire or light. Fire consumes and purifies. For example, fire is used to "kosherize" metal objects that were used with non-kosher foods. The pagans and ancient Christians used fire to purify the souls of those deemed impure. Once fire consumes its target, it ceases to exist. Light, however, spreads and gains strength as it illuminates the darkness.

There is a dispute in the *Mishnah* regarding the order of the Chanukah lighting. According to the school of Shamai, we start by lighting eight lights on the first night and decrease by one light each night until we are left with one light on the eighth night. According to the school of Hillel, we start by lighting one light on the first night and increase by one light each night until we light eight on the eighth night.

According to Shamai, the Chanukah lights represent the aggressive, yet purifying, attributes of fire. In order to save the Jewish people from spiritual destruction, the Maccabees had to destroy the Syrian-Greek armies, liberate the Temple by force, and destroy the vestiges of Hellenistic culture in Israel. According to Shamai, who almost always propagates a stringent view regarding Jewish law, Chanukah represents the idea of cleansing and purifying ourselves from those things that take us away from Judaism. At the beginning of the holiday we need the full force and fervor of the fires of purification. At the end, having succeeded, we only require a single flame.

According to Hillel the Chanukah lights represent the growth and spreading of *Torah* despite the trials and tribulations thrust upon us by our oppressors and the exile. The Jews under the yoke of the Hellenists started off weak in their faith and commitment but, with the encouragement and leadership of the Maccabees, grew strong both physically and spiritually until they were able to throw off the Hellenistic influences and return to *Torah*. The gradual increase of lights on Chanukah represents this spiritual growth. By the eighth day we are strong enough to continue growing spiritually by the light of our faith.

We follow the opinion of Hillel.

CHANUKAH – *Making Miracles*

Every holiday on the Jewish calendar not only commemorates a past event but also indicates a period of time propitious for the occurrence of that particular form of event. For example, Passover not only commemorates the Exodus but also indicates that the period of Passover is a time of redemption. The holiday of Chanukah therefore is not only commemorative of the miracles that occurred then but also indicative of the miracles that can occur every year at that time.

The chassidic master Rabbi Levi Yitzchak of Berditchev categorizes miracles as those that are completely initiated from the heavenly realm and those that are initiated or "pulled down" from the physical world. For example, the splitting of the Sea of Reeds during the Exodus was purely a heavenly initiative since, according to the *Midrash*, the Jews were no more deserving of a miracle based on their merits than were the Egyptians. The Jews played absolutely no part in bringing about that miracle.

The miraculous events of Chanukah, including the military victory against the Syrian-Greeks, were initiated by the actions of the Jews. Led by the Maccabees the Jews took the first step by fighting for their religious liberty. When God saw their effort and sacrifice, He performed miracles for them. The Jews "pulled down" miracles with their actions and deeds.

Reflections

Chanukah is a time ripe for miracles. It is uniquely special in that it allows us to actually initiate actions that can cause miracles to be "pulled down" from above. Chanukah gives us the power to make spectacular things happen in our own lives and in the world in which we live. It's up to us to take the first step to make amazing things happen.

CHANUKAH - *Seeing Miracles*

We commemorate two miracles on Chanukah. The first and more popular miracle is that a one day supply of oil burned for eight days. The second miracle is the victory of the greatly outnumbered Jewish fighters, the Maccabees, over the mighty Syrian-Greek armies. We commemorate the miracle of the oil by lighting Menorahs in our windows to publicize this great miracle to the world. We make no mention of the military miracle. In our prayers we mention the military miracle in a special insert in the silent devotion (*Al Hanisim*) without mentioning the miracle of the oil. The question is obvious. Why only publicize the miracle of the oil while confining the military miracle to our private and silent prayers?

The miracle of the oil is a scientifically provable event. A certain amount of oil can only burn a certain amount of time. When a one day supply of oil burns for eight days everyone must agree that it is a miracle. A military victory can never conclusively be attributed to any one event since many factors can determine the outcome of a battle including quality and type of weaponry, training, motivation, physical conditioning, climate – the list is endless. When viewing the Jewish victory, the world can deny any miraculous occurrence and attribute the victory to hundreds of subjective factors. We, however, recognize that the victory was miraculous.

In 1967 the Israeli Army destroyed the combined armies of at least six Arab countries and liberated Jerusalem, Judea, Samaria, the Golan, Sinai, and Gaza with relatively minimal casualties in just six days. As unbelievable as that sounds the world still attributes the Six Day War victory to factors such as weapons, training, and motivation. Only the Jewish people realize and recognize the victory for what it was: a miracle.

Therefore on Chanukah we publicize to the world the miracle that they cannot deny, the miracle of the oil. Privately, however, we commemorate the military victory, the miracle that only people of faith can recognize.

Reflections

Being Jewish means recognizing the not so obvious miracles that God performs in the world on a daily basis. All you need to do is open your eyes and look around, and you'll find them. May we be blessed to recognize the miracles in our lives and to appreciate them.

CHANUKAH - *Keeping the Flame*

I once had the honor and privilege of hearing Rabbi J.B. Soloveitchik address a group of high school students on a tour of Yeshiva University during the Chanukah season. The Rav spoke to them about the importance of the message of Chanukah. The following is my attempt at summarizing and understanding the Rav's teaching.

Chanukah is the only Jewish holiday that is not based on a biblical source text, yet it is one of the most widely celebrated and beloved holidays, celebrated for close to 2500 years. The only authoritative source we have for Chanukah is found in the Talmud, the Oral Law.

The holiday of Chanukah is a testament to the power of the Oral Law and the rabbinic tradition passed on from generation to generation. In fact, the events leading up to the miracle of Chanukah were part of a battle between Jewish tradition and Hellenism. The Hellenists, both Greek and Jewish, believed solely in the power of the physical. Physical beauty, strength, and wealth were the hallmarks and idolatry of their culture. Judaism, however, stressed inner beauty, kindness, spirituality, and modesty, based on an unbroken tradition given to Moses and the Jewish people at Mt. Sinai.

Part of the miracle of Chanukah was that faith and spirituality triumphed over materialism and hedonism. The fact that Chanukah has no textual source underscores and emphasizes this very message.

Chanukah celebrates the power of Jewish tradition and the eternity of the *Torah*, both oral and written. Every time we light those holy candles and celebrate those great victories and miracles, we count ourselves as a link in that unbroken chain of Jewish tradition, and guarantee its continuation.

May we be strengthened with the power of our holy ancestors to keep the flame of our *Torah* and traditions burning brighter and stronger than ever.

CHANUKAH – *The Ninth Day*

At a *Shabbat* dinner on the eighth night of Chanukah someone at the table mentioned that a co-worker had asked her what occurred on the ninth day of Chanukah. While everyone at the table laughed at the innocent absurdity of the question, I saw in it a deep lesson.

It's often easy to feel excited, joyous, and spiritually charged during the celebration of a holiday. Whether it is the *Menorah* on Chanukah, the Seder on Pesach, or the Succah on Succot, the "props" of each holiday help get us into the appropriate frame of mind for that particular holiday. We immerse ourselves in the laws and customs of the holidays and thereby attain a level of spiritual excitement greater than during the rest of the year. The real test of our spiritual growth, however, is not how we are during the holiday but rather how we are when the holiday is over.

The eight days are Chanukah are days when we feel the light of freedom and *Torah* fill our spirits as we gaze upon the lights of the *Menorah*. But what happens on the ninth day, when we no longer light the *Menorah*? Do we still feel spiritually uplifted? Are we still committed to growing religiously and spiritually? Will we still be able to see the miracles that surround us on a daily basis?

The real message of Chanukah is not to see the miraculous and to spread the light of *Torah* and freedom for eight days. Rather, it is to take that message and apply it to the ninth, tenth, eleventh, and to everyday of our lives.

SHKALIM – *Part of Something Bigger*

The *Parsha* of *Shkalim* is always read before the holiday of Purim. This *Parsha* commands every Jew to contribute a half shekel to the Temple. In our own day, even without the Temple in Jerusalem, we remember this *Mitzvah* by donating the equivalent of a half shekel to charity on Purim.

Why is every Jew required to donate exactly one half shekel to fulfill this particular *Mitzvah* and why is this *Mitzvah* connected to Purim?

The number "one" represents completeness, unity, and self sufficiency. In Judaism there is only one number one. We say it twice daily in the Shema. "Hear Israel. God is our God. God is One." Only God can be one. Only God can be totally complete and self sufficient. Human beings need to grow and constantly work on themselves to become better. Human beings need to connect with others to reach their potential. Therefore we are commanded to give half of a shekel to remind us that we are part of a greater whole. We need to be part of a community to reach our potential and become complete. We are all halves. Only God is whole.

On Purim we celebrate the salvation of the Jewish People from the hands of the evil Haman. According to the Megillah the Jews took part in the celebrations of the Kingdom and even drank from the vessels taken as booty from the destroyed Temple in Jerusalem. They must have done this unknowingly for no Jew would ever knowingly dare defile the holy vessels. They didn't know they were drinking from holy vessels because they had forgotten about Jerusalem and their heritage. They were so happy to be accepted by the royalty and society of Persia and so at home in their new land that they forgot who they were and where they came from. They were too drunk, both literally and figuratively, to know what they were doing or what was happening to them. They had no idea that Haman was planning to wipe out every Jew in the world.

Right before the fateful day of destruction the Jews were awakened by Mordechai and Esther to come together in prayer and fasting for three days. Only when they joined together as one nation were they saved.

Only when they realized that they were all just half shekels, a part of a greater whole, were they rescued without even a drop of Jewish blood being spilled.

Reflections

We are living in times very similar to the days of the Purim story. Let's not get so drunk that we forget who we are and what our purpose is. Let's not only give the half shekel, but let's become the half shekel and join together with the community to form a unified whole.

ZACHOR

There is a *Mitzvah* in the *Torah* for every Jew to remember that the nation of Amelak attacked the Jews soon after their exodus from Egypt. Every year, on the *Shabbat* preceding Purim, we read the portion of the *Torah,* called *Zachor,* which recounts that episode to fulfill this *Mitzvah.* Why is it so important to remember the evil of Amalek to the extent that the *Torah* actually commands us to do it? What is the connection between this *Mitzvah* and Purim?

There are two other *Mitzvot* of remembrance in the *Torah.* The first is to remember the *Shabbat,* which we fulfill by reciting *Kiddush* on Friday night. The second is to remember the exodus from Egypt, which we fulfill by reciting the Shema and other prayers. Both of these events are foundations of our religion and both represent positive events and experiences. They represent gifts given to the Jewish People by God. The reason why the *Torah* needs to specifically command us to remember these events is perhaps because people tend to forget favors done for them. A person is initially thankful to a favor giver but after some time passes the event blurs and the benefactor is often forgotten. However, when a person receives a beating, he never forgets the pain and humiliation. Why then do we need a commandment to remember Amalek? How can we ever forget the beating and humiliation?!

The answer is sad but true. For over a thousand years Jews have been beaten and murdered by Christians for having allegedly killed their deity. Yet today that very same "passion play" that instigated the horrors is being shown to millions and praised by critics as a work of art. My father recounts how the gentiles of the small Polish town of his childhood would emerge from their churches on Sundays after listening to their priests preach about how the Jews killed Jesus, and beat up Jews in the streets. Sure, not every Pole actually beat up Jews but then not every Nazi physically pulled the trigger either. How can the world have forgotten the crimes and horrors of even just the last century?

The saddest part is that we too have forgotten the past. We sit by in a fog of security while anti-Semitism raises its ugly head throughout the world. We read about our brothers and sisters suffering in Israel and just complain about how scary it is to visit, and fly to Florida instead. We place our trust in Congress and the Constitution instead of in God and the *Torah*. This is what the Jews did in the Purim story. They trusted in Ahashverosh, but were reawakened by Haman. Let's make sure we always remember our past sufferings so that we can assure that they never reoccur. This is the *Mitzvah* of *Zachor*.

PURIM – *A Reminder*

The Talmud teaches that after the Messiah brings the final redemption all of the Jewish festivals will be abolished except for Purim. The reason given is that the festivals all commemorate events and miracles relating to the Exodus, which will be overshadowed by the miraculous events surrounding the Messianic Era. Why, then, will the miracle of Purim not be overshadowed as well?

It is important to remember the past for two major reasons. Firstly, by studying the past we can make sure to avoid repeating mistakes. Secondly, by analyzing our history we can learn lessons to help us grow. The greatest lessons often come out of misfortune and tragedy. By remembering these, not only can we assure that they are not repeated, but we can also appreciate our good fortune that much more.

After our initial redemption from Egyptian slavery we needed to recall our past misfortunes to really appreciate our freedom. Now that we find ourselves in this two thousand year Roman exile our tragedies, including the Holocaust, have far surpassed those of Egypt. When the Messiah will finally bring us redemption we will need to study the history of our own tragic exile.

The story of Purim represents our experience in this exile. The Megillah is ambiguous about the exact date of the events contained within it to teach us that they can and do occur in almost any time period throughout our exile. The heroes of the story are everyday people who stand up to take their places as saviors of the Jewish People, much like those individuals in every generation who rise from mediocrity to lead extraordinary lives of accomplishment. The villains of the story are also stereotypical of the evil oppressors who arise in every generation and attempt to wipe the Jews off the face of the earth. The setting and circumstances are also quite common. The Jews become comfortable and secure in a foreign land only to discover that, overnight, they are an enemy requiring destruction. When salvation finally comes it arrives through the hands of righteous gentiles, with the Jewish heroes exerting their influence behind the scenes. Most importantly, just as

God's name is hidden in the Purim story, so too does He remain hidden throughout the Jewish sojourn in exile.

Therefore, Purim will be the only holiday remaining after the arrival of the Messiah because it is the story of, and the testament to, Jewish survival in the exile, which we must study and learn from forever.

PURIM - *Accepting the Torah*

The Sages of the Talmud teach that, after their salvation from Haman, the Jews wholeheartedly accepted the *Torah* in a way different from their acceptance of it at Sinai (*Kiymu v'kiblu*). Whereas at Sinai the Jews were forced to accept the *Torah*, which is based on a *Midrash* that God held the mountain over their heads like a barrel and gave them the choice of accepting the *Torah* or death, in Persia they did so willingly. This second acceptance of *Torah* would be everlasting.

According to this teaching, the actions of somewhat assimilated Jews living in Persian exile was greater than those of the great generation of the wilderness that witnessed the miracles of the Exodus and revelation. Why is this so? The *Torah* clearly states that, at Sinai, the Jews accepted the *Torah* with the momentous words, "*Naaseh Ve Nishma* – We will do and hear," which indicated their devotion to following its laws even before understanding them thoroughly. How, then, can we understand the teaching of our Sages cited above?

The Jews at Sinai had just left a life of horrible persecution and slavery. Their perception of the "outside" world was defined by their experience. A world filled with cruelty, violence, and paganism did not appeal to them. At the same time the Jews were witness to the greatest miracles ever performed including the ten plagues, the splitting of the sea, and finally, the magnificent revelation at Sinai. They were presented with a moral code unparalleled in the ancient world by God Himself, while isolated in the wilderness with nowhere else to go. How could they possibly not accept it? When the Sages say that they were "forced" to accept the *Torah* they really meant that they had absolutely no logical alternative to accepting it.

The Jews in Persia were in an almost completely opposite position. They were full members of one of the greatest empires of history. They faced no persecution and were even invited to participate in the royal court and celebrations. On the other hand, they had no prophets to lead them and they witnessed no miracles to inspire them. Instead, they found themselves facing total annihilation. Even their salvation came about in a hidden manner, much differently than the miracles of the Exodus.

Based on their situation in Persia the Jews had no logical reason compelling them to accept the *Torah*. Yet, they embraced the *Torah* with love and even added a new holiday with new commandments: Purim. This acceptance, coming solely out of faith and love, was seen as being more significant than the acceptance at Sinai.

In our own day and age we find ourselves in a similar situation as the Jews of Persia. When we accept the *Torah* and Judaism we do so not out of fear or distress. We do so because we truly believe that the *Torah* is God's truth given to us as a precious gift. We have all the choices and opportunities in the world. Let's choose to embrace our *Torah* and heritage just like our ancestors did 2500 years ago in Persia.

PURIM – *Drastic Change*

The Jewish calendar is a cycle that repeats itself every year. The Jewish holidays represent particular attributes or "energies" of that cycle, as opposed to simply commemorating historical events. For example, the time period of Pesach represents redemption. Therefore every time that period occurs during the year the energy of redemption is strong and the time is "ripe" for redemption to occur. Rosh Hashanah is always a time of Judgment. Yom Kippur is always a time of atonement. The same holds true for all of the holidays.

What is the particular energy of Purim? The answer lies in the main theme of the holiday. What then is the main theme of Purim?

The first place to look is the actual holiday name. Purim literally means lottery, representing the lots that Haman drew to decide on which date to liquidate the Jews. Why name the holiday after a lottery? Hold on to this question for later.

The next place to look in our search for the main theme of Purim is the name of the holiday's hero, Esther. Although the name Esther is at first glance just a Persian name, our Rabbis teach that it has a much deeper and significant meaning. The Hebrew root of Esther is the word meaning hidden or secret. The Rabbis teach that this idea of "hidden" refers to a concept called *Hester Panim,* which literally means "the hiding of the face". This concept of *Hester Panim* is used to refer to the idea that God relates to the world in a hidden manner. God is operating but man doesn't realize it because it looks like God really isn't there at all. For example, when God took the Jews out of Egypt and then split the sea for them, it was obvious to the world that God was performing miracles. The "hand" of God was revealed. When the Israeli army utterly destroyed the Arab armies in just six days God's hand was hidden to anyone not actually on the battlefield allowing the world to say that the victory was due to anything but God. This is the idea of *Hester Panim*, the hiding of the face. The tradition of wearing costumes on Purim is the active way of representing this *Hester Panim*.

God was relating to the world with *Hester Panim* during the Purim story. The Jews were leading a comfortable life in the exile of the

Persian Empire. Their leader Mordechai held a prominent post in the royal palace and they were even invited to partake in the royal banquet thrown by King Ahashverosh. By what seemed to be a random twist of fate Esther was chosen as queen of the empire. Then suddenly, in the blink of an eye, everything changed when Haman convinced the King to wipe out the Jewish nation for no reason. One day they were feasting in the palace and the next they were preparing for an unprecedented holocaust.

The Jews were awakened by their impending doom. They prayed and fasted, and Esther risked her life to appear before the King to beg for the lives of her people. As suddenly as the evil decree was created, it was destroyed. The world turned upside down. Instead of being massacred, the Jews fought back and routed their enemies. What was to be the day of destruction for the Jews turned into a great day of rejoicing and rededication to the *Torah*.

Throughout the drama God is hidden. Events seem to be happening in a random and coincidental manner, much like a lottery. This is why the holiday is called "lottery". *Hester Panim*. The energy of the holiday is the revealing of the hidden.

Passover - *It's Time Again*

What is the special energy of Passover and how does it relate to the holiday preceding it, Purim, and the holiday following it, Shavuot?

Passover is the holiday that commemorates the redemption of the Jews from Egypt and the rebirth of the Jewish nation as we know it today. Therefore, the energy of Passover is redemption and rebirth. It is no coincidence that Passover always must occur at the beginning of spring, the season of the rebirth and redemption of nature. When we celebrate the Seder we are supposed to feel as though we ourselves are being redeemed from Egypt.

The energy of Purim is "hidden" or "Chaos". Every part of the holiday represents these energies from the name of the holiday (*Pur* or Lottery-Chaos) to the name of the main character (Esther - hidden) to the absence of God's name in the megillah. Purim occurs in the winter when the air of redemption is hidden in the cold and darkness. It carries with it a sense of confusion and even hopelessness. It comes right before Passover because our Rabbis teach that the Jews in Egypt were on the forty ninth level of impurity (fifty is the worst) immediately before their redemption. Often a person reaches the lowest levels of confusion and despair before the redemption comes in the blink of an eye to lift him out of the darkness into the light.

As we approach Passover we should be aware that even if things seem dark and hopeless today our own personal redemption awaits us just around the corner. Just like the Jews went from slavery to freedom in a matter of minutes so to can our own situations change as suddenly. Only after we experience our own personal redemption can we be ready to experience the energy of accepting the *Torah* on *Shavuot*.

DAYENU – *Is it Enough?*

Every Passover we sing a beautiful song towards the end of the Seder. The refrain of the song is "*Dayenu*" which means "it would be enough for us". The song enumerates the great miracles performed for the Jewish people from the Exodus until their entrance into the Land of Israel and after each one proclaims "*Dayenu*". For example, "If God had just taken us out of Egypt but not split the sea, that would have been enough for us".

The obvious question regarding "*Dayenu*" is, would it really have been enough? Would it have been enough if God took us out of Egypt but did not split the sea or if God had split the sea but had not brought us to Mt. Sinai or given us the *Torah*? For example, if you gave me a brand new car but didn't give me the keys, would that be enough? Of course not! Then what does this song really mean?

The *Dayenu* is a love song written by the Jewish people to God, their beloved. In fact, most of the psalms and prayers that we recite should be viewed as love songs and poems to a beloved. This is also why it is the custom of many to recite the Song of Songs, the ultimate love song between God and the Jewish People, after the Seder.

When a person is in love with someone every moment spent with their beloved is precious to them. Of course they would rather have that moment last a lifetime, yet they are willing to accept even just a moment to be with them. Every moment with them is so precious that it stands alone in importance regardless of what the next moment might bring.

The Jewish People are so in love with God that every moment in His presence is precious to them. Although we hope and yearn for the full redemption we still cherish and treasure every step towards that goal. Although we continue to strive for more we rejoice in every moment of love that God grants us. This is the true meaning of *Dayenu*.

With this new understanding of *Dayenu* we can reach a more meaningful understanding of the entire Seder and possibly the entire *Torah*. If our relationship with God is comparable to a relationship between lovers then every *Mitzvah* that we perform is really an act of love. All love relationships have low points when we feel distant from or apathetic towards our lover, but true love overcomes these downswings and remains as strong as ever. So too our relationship with God remains forever strong even if we sometimes feel distant and "unloved".

MATZAH – *Freedom or Slavery*

The main theme of the Passover Seder is freedom, and all the rituals we perform during it represent either that freedom, or the slavery that preceded it. For example, the wine we drink and the way we drink it, reclining, represent freedom, while the Maror represents slavery. What exactly does the Matzah represent? On the one hand it is referred to as the bread of the poor or the bread of affliction, while on the other hand it is meant to represent our speedy deliverance from slavery to freedom and is eaten while reclining in a festive manner.

There is really no contradiction between the "poor" bread and the bread of freedom. To understand why, we need to delve deeper into the concept of freedom. In modern society freedom is commonly associated with wealth or material comfort. Our image of free men at the Seder usually takes the form of rich men enjoying an extravagant feast in an opulent setting. Our *Torah* has a different image of wealth and freedom. The Sages of the *Mishnah* teach that the wealthy man is one who is satisfied with his lot, and that the free man is one who studies *Torah*.

Although the *Torah* mandates that people support themselves through honest and diligent labor, it does not mandate the pursuit of wealth at the expense of family, personal growth, relationships, and religious observance. Practically every one of the great Rabbis of the *Mishnah* and Talmud and throughout the Middle Ages, including the great commentators Rashi and Rambam, engaged in a meaningful profession to earn a living. These professions ranged from shoemaker and tanner to scientist and doctor. However, it is clear from their writings that these men considered their professions as only a means to allow them to live a life of spirituality and *Torah* study. They worked for only a small part of the day and spent the majority of their time engaged in *Torah* study and *Mitzvot*.

Almost all of us spend most of our time engaged in a pursuit of wealth that leaves us practically no time to engage in the *Torah* pursuits that are the true purpose of our sojourn in this life. We do this because we think that our freedom depends on it. Without wealth we feel as though we are worthless failures.

The Matzah teaches us that even the bread of the poor can be the symbol of freedom, because freedom is not how much you have but how you live your life and how you view yourself. Pesach is a time when we should think about what freedom means to us and how we can achieve it in a way that reflects its true meaning instead of how it is defined by society. May God give us all the strength to be truly free.

PLAGUES VS. SEA SPLITTING

According to Jewish tradition the miracle of the splitting of the Sea of Reeds occurred on the seventh day of Passover. The miracle of the "splitting" holds a much greater position of importance than do the ten plagues wrought against the Egyptians. Several paragraphs of the Haggadah, read at the Seder, are dedicated to proving this by pointing out the five to one advantage in the number of miracles performed at the sea over those performed in Egypt. Why was the miracle of the splitting greater than the miracle of the plagues, and why do we make such a point of highlighting that fact?

There are three reasons. The first is uniquely designed to fit our modern view of morality. Whereas the plagues effected the entire Egyptian population the miracle of the splitting solely effected the military. There were no civilian casualties. Therefore, we are eager to highlight this purely "military" victory. As an aside, even this "military" victory is played down, for the Talmud teaches that when the angels began to sing the Hallel after the destruction of the Egyptian army at the sea God rebuked them be saying, "how can you sing while my creations are drowning in the sea?" Therefore, to this day we do not recite the complete Hallel on the latter days of Passover. The second reason is that each of the ten plagues could conceivably be explained as occurring as a result of natural, albeit unusual, causes. This, in fact, is partially why Pharaoh finds the irrational courage to ignore the message behind the plagues. Maybe they were just caused by an aberration of nature, as oppose to the hand of an invisible God? The splitting of the sea, however, was clearly a miracle. At the very moment that the Jewish nation was at the edge of the water with the Egyptians bearing down on them, the sea split long enough for them to pass through, and then returned to drown the Egyptians. There was absolutely no denying the miracle at the sea.

The third reason is, I think, the most powerful. The Jews played absolutely no part in the miracle of the plagues. They were simply bystanders, silent witnesses to the might of God. At the sea, however, the Jews had to actually instigate the miracle. According to the *Midrash* it was only after Nachshon Ben Aminadav walked into the sea, proving that he and the rest of the people were ready and willing to sacrifice their lives, that the sea finally split. Part of the greatness of the miracle, then, was that the Jews played a part in it by showing their loyalty and their faith.

PESACH – *Sea Splitting*

According to tradition the Jews passed through the split Sea of Reeds on the seventh day of Passover. During the prayer service of that day we only recite an abridged version of the Hallel, the prayer commemorating a festive or miraculous event that we say on the other Festivals. One of the reasons given is that we diminish our rejoicing in deference to the death and suffering of the Egyptians at the sea. There is, I think, an even deeper reason for abridging the Hallel.

The rejoicing on the other Festivals is a result of much hard work done by the Jews to raise themselves to a higher level of spirituality and holiness. The rejoicing on Shavuot comes after forty nine days of spiritual ascension and the rejoicing of Succot comes after the repentance and rebirth of the High Holidays. Therefore, the Hallel that is appropriate for these days is a complete one. The salvation that the Jews experienced at the Sea of Reeds was not the result of great spiritual growth of merit. On the contrary, God commands Moses to tell the Jews not to pray but to just go forward into the waters. The prayers of the Jews would be of no help to them at that moment. The Jews were in a state of shock and horror as they watched the Egyptian army bearing down on them and the sea blocking their only means of escape. They were still on such a low level of spirituality as a result of their slavery that they lacked the merit to ensure the success of their prayers. The only option left to them was to prove their loyalty to God with their bodies and jump into the sea. It was this show of faith that caused their salvation. They did not, however, merit reciting the full Hallel as on other festivals because they did not gain their salvation through spiritual merit or holiness.

The Rabbis teach that even the lowliest handmaid of the Jews merited seeing the greatest prophetic visions at the splitting of the sea. Even though, as postulated above, the Jews did not merit salvation through spiritual merit, they nevertheless reached the greatest spiritual and holy heights as a result of their simple and total faith. By jumping into the sea the Jews accomplished more than they could ever do with prayer. They literally put their lives on the line and proved their worthiness for salvation.

The Talmud compares the difficulty of earning a livelihood and finding a mate to the splitting of the sea. The meaning of this is now clear. These pursuits require us to completely throw ourselves into them with almost blind faith to succeed. Only by showing our total faith can we hope to merit success in these endeavors.

HAGGADAH – *How to Answer*

When the wise one of the four sons in the Haggadah inquires as to the nature of the laws and practices of Passover, we answer by teaching him the law that prohibits anything to be eaten after the afikomen. Why is this particular, relatively minor, law chosen as the answer?

A simple explanation is that we actually teach the wise son all of the laws of Passover, but only mention the afikomen since it is the last ritual we perform at the Seder and signifies the completion of all of the laws preceding it.

I think there is an incredibly insightful explanation hidden in the afikomen. The afikomen is translated as dessert, since it is eaten at the conclusion of the meal on a full stomach. Dessert conjures up images of delicious tasting sweets that bring joy and satisfaction to the diner. When attempting to bring someone closer to Judaism and *Torah* we must present them with the afikomen, the sweetest parts of our heritage that will make them smile and beg for more. This is the only way to excite Jews about Judaism. Not by immediately inundating them with all of the prohibitions, but by showing them the beauty and sweetness. The afikomen.

OMER – *Always New*

There is a *Mitzvah* to count the forty nine days between the first day of Passover and Shavuot. It is also a *Mitzvah* to recite a blessing before counting each night. Since the counting is really one *Mitzvah* spread over forty nine days, with each subsequent night's count depending on the previous one, shouldn't we only make one blessing at the beginning of the first nights count to cover the entire *Mitzvah*?

The counting of the Omer represents the growth process that we are supposed to engage in to prepare ourselves to receive the *Torah* on Shavuot. There are two aspects to growth. One is continuity and connection to a solid foundation. That foundation consists of basic beliefs and faith arrived at through careful consideration and exploration. It is a struggle to build that solid foundation necessary to grow in spirituality and observance. Once that foundation is built, however, the struggle does not end. That's where the second aspect of growth comes into play.

The second aspect of growth is freshness. As strong as the original foundation might be it will become boring and stale if it is not constantly used, updated, and examined. The Rabbis teach that the *Torah* should be as fresh in our eyes as if we are seeing it for the first time every day. Staleness and boredom can only be detrimental to, or can even reverse, growth.

Therefore, the blessing before the counting of the Omer each day represents the constant rejuvenation and reinvigoration that we should strive to experience in our growth process towards acceptance of *Torah*. Each new day should not only reaffirm our existing beliefs and convictions, but should lead us to re-explore and re-examine our *Torah* study and observance and find new ways to experience and enjoy them.

PESACH SHENI – *Second Chances*

According to the Halacha, only Jews that are "*tahor* – ritually fit" can take part in the Pesach offering. Those Jews who were not *tahor* during the first Pesach after the exodus beseeched Moses to allow them to offer a belated Pesach offering. Moses asked God, and was commanded to allow those Jews who were either unfit or legitimately unable to offer the first Pesach the opportunity to offer a second one exactly one month following the original event. This *Mitzvah*, known as *Pesach Sheni* (second Pesach), is the only example of "making up" a *Mitzvah*. It doesn't apply, however, to those who intentionally avoid the offering. Why was the *Mitzvah* of Pesach, as opposed to the other 612, the only one chosen to have the honor of being "made up" if missed?

Celebrating American independence on August 4th instead of July 4th seems foolish. Why doesn't this hold true for celebrating Pesach, which represents Jewish independence from Egyptian slavery, a month late?

When a person is unable to perform a particular *Mitzvah* their soul suffers from disappointment and guilt. These negative feelings last only until the person performs another *Mitzvah*, the performance of which nourishes the soul and creates feelings of spiritual satisfaction and fulfillment.

The *Mitzvah* of *Pesach* is unique since it represents the birth of the Jewish nation, and therefore, relates not only to the spiritual but also to the nationalistic and patriotic aspirations of the soul. Nationalism and patriotism are among the most powerful forces that drive civilization. Man is willing do sacrifice everything, including his life, for a flag. How many hundreds of millions of people have perished in wars fought over national sovereignty? How many sacrifice their personal comfort based on patriotism?

Those unable to participate in the *Mitzvah* of *Pesach* felt unpatriotic and separated from the rest of the nation. This feeling of alienation was more powerful than any disappointment stemming from the non performance of a *Mitzvah*. It threatened to destroy their identity as members of the Jewish nation. This is why it was so important to allow them the opportunity to partake in the *Pesach*, even a month late.

Shavuot – *Receiving the Torah*

Shavuot is the only holiday in the *Torah* that does not have an exact date ascribed to it. The date for *Shavuot* every year is determined, according to *Torah* law, by counting forty nine days from Passover, with the fiftieth being *Shavuot*. There is a powerful message to be learned from this.

Shavuot commemorates the receiving of the *Torah*. The *Torah* could only be received by a nation prepared to receive it. The Jews were not ready to receive the *Torah* right after leaving Egypt. Only after forty nine days of growth and preparation were they finally deemed ready.

Shavuot represents each individual's personal acceptance of the *Torah*, which can only come about through growth and preparation. Every person grows at a different pace. There's no uniform deadline for the culmination of that growth that can be imposed upon the Jews as a group. Each person must receive the *Torah* when they are ready and prepared, and not before. Only then will the receiving be permanent.

Reflections

Jumping into something too quickly is almost always a bad idea. Relationships that start off at an extreme level of intensity and passion often fizzle out once the initial excitement is over. A relationship should obviously contain excitement and passion, but it should also progress gradually, allowing the participants to get to know each other and develop real feelings for each other that will stand the test of time. The same is true for spirituality and religious observance. Too much too fast is a recipe for burnout. Spiritual and religious growth requires thought, experience, and study to be long lasting and successful. It takes time and lots of hard work.

TORAH STUDY – *The True Objective*

A story is told of a king who wanted to bequeath his kingdom to his three sons. To test their loyalty the king called them to the throne room and presented them with the following task, which if completed successfully would assure each of them a part of the kingdom. He gave each son a bucket and told them to draw water from the well and carry it over to a trough some 100 feet away, and to keep repeating the task until he told them to stop.

The sons went to the well and eagerly filled their buckets with water. When they began carrying the buckets to the trough they realized that the buckets had holes in them. By the time they reached the trough there were only a few drops of water remaining, the rest having spilled through the holes. Two of the brothers threw down their buckets and quit, claiming that their father was certainly playing a joke on them by giving them faulty buckets, and they refused to be fooled by him. The third brother, however, continued drawing water from the well and carrying it to the trough where he deposited the few remaining drops. He kept performing this task for the entire day until, finally, the king sent word for them to stop and appear before him with their buckets.

With his sons lined up before him the king asked them to present their buckets. The two sons laughed, proclaiming that they had not fallen for their father's joke and had not wasted their time performing the silly task. The king then examined the third son's bucket and proclaimed him the sole heir to the inheritance. The other two sons were furious. The buckets had holes in them! There was no way that the third son came anywhere close to filling up the trough!

The king explained that the true purpose of the task was not for them to fill up the trough but rather to clean out the buckets. Only the third son who continued drawing water fulfilled the mission.

The same is true regarding the study of *Torah*, which is often compared to water. Although breadth of knowledge is valuable and many times necessary for proper performance of *mitzvot*, the main purpose of *Torah* study is to clean out or purify our minds, bodies, hearts, and souls.

Reflections

The *Torah* that we study penetrates the depths of our souls and transforms and elevates them, and us, to greater heights of wisdom, spirituality and holiness. Therefore, we shouldn't get discouraged if we are unable to complete a predetermined amount of material or master a certain subject. The amount of *Torah* knowledge mastered is not the primary gauge of success. The important thing is to set aside as much time as possible to engage in the study of *Torah* on a regular basis. Doing so will insure our continued growth and success as Jews and as ethical and moral members of society.

THREE WEEKS – *Can We Cry?*

According to Jewish law and tradition the three weeks beginning on the seventeenth day of the month of Tammuz and culminating with the fast of the ninth of the month of Av (*Tisha B'av*) are observed as a time of mourning for the destruction of Jerusalem and the temple and countless other tragedies throughout Jewish history. Many customs of mourning are observed during this period to help us feel the sadness and tragedy and to inspire us to repentance.

How do we who, thank God, live in a free and prosperous country and maintain a comfortable lifestyle feel the tragedy and loss of the destruction of the Temple? From where can we draw the tears to shed in mourning?

The story is told of a family in a tiny Russian shtetl, whose young son had fallen deathly ill. The doctors gave the boy no chance of recovery. In desperation the father decided to travel to Poland to visit a Hasidic Rebbe renown for performing miracles. After a difficult three week journey by wagon, the man arrived in the Polish town and went directly to the Rebbe's house of study, and waited several hours to see the Rebbe in private. The Rebbe listened compassionately to the man's story and then retired to his private chamber for a half hour. When he emerged, the Rebbe told the man that he had left no stone unturned in the heavenly chambers but that there was nothing that he could do to help the man's son. The judgment was sealed.

The man was distraught, but accepted the Rebbe's decision as final, thanked him for his help, and got back on his wagon for the journey back home. As he was nearing the town limits the man heard someone screaming for him to stop. He turned around to see the Rebbe running after the wagon. He stopped the wagon and the Rebbe climbed aboard and began apologizing profusely. The man tried to stop him.

"Rebbe, I know that you did everything that you could to help my son but it just wasn't part of the heavenly decree. You have nothing to apologize for". The Rebbe answered, "You are right that I could not change the heavenly decree, but there is something that I should have done. I should have cried with you, because when a Jew is crying it is the responsibility of every Jew to cry with him."

The Rebbe sat with the man and cried. Both men sat on that wagon and cried from the depths of their souls. At that moment the gates of heaven opened and the decree was torn up. When the man returned home he was greeted by his son, in perfect health.

Even if we have the good fortune of not feeling the tears of mourning and sadness in our own lives, we know that there are so many Jews who live in fear or persecution, who face danger every day, who suffer from illness, poverty and heartache. When a Jew is crying it is the responsibility of every Jew to cry with him. We have plenty to cry about during these three weeks, if not for ourselves, then for our brothers and sisters.

May God hear our cries and bring us the salvation we all need.

GREETING ON TISHA B'AV

One of the things that we refrain from doing during the first half of *Tisha B'av* is greeting people. We don't say, "Hello, how are you?" This is a strange custom. What is so bad about asking someone how he or she is doing? Why is it so opposed to the mourning character of the day?

On *Tisha B'av* a Jew is in a total state of depression and despair. He is preoccupied with mourning and sadness and simply does not have the desire or even capability to interact in a friendly and caring way with another person, even a close friend. We all have periods of time when we feel this way. During these times we avoid contact with other people for fear that we will not have the ability to properly interact with them. The first part of *Tisha B'av* is one of those times for every Jew. We are all in mourning and cannot be expected to engage in friendly interpersonal interactions.

Another way of looking at this custom is as follows. It is very painful to see someone you love and care about and not be able to greet them. There could be many different reasons why you would not be able to speak to them, but the result is always painful. On *Tisha B'av* we force ourselves to experience this pain as part of our mourning and sadness. It is the same pain of loneliness and alienation that we experience when feeling distant from God. It is the pain of exile.

KRIYAH ON TISHA B'AV

Many of the prohibitions and customs relating to the day of *Tisha B'av* are the same that relate to a mourner. For example, we sit on the floor and refrain from greeting people. Why then do we not tear our garments -- *Kriyah*, one of the most fundamental signs of intense mourning, on Tisha B'av?

One possible answer is that *Kriyah* is too intense a form of mourning. Soon after the destruction of the Second Temple the sages sought to establish a uniform set of rules for mourning the destruction. Some sages felt that eating meat and drinking wine should be completely forbidden. The majority of the sages, however, felt that completely prohibiting meat and wine would simply be too intense, and would plunge the Jewish People into a state of constant mourning and depression. These sages understood that life must go on, so they confined the intense mourning period in which meat and wine are prohibited to the week directly preceding the fast of *Tisha B'av*. *Kriyah* is such an intense physical act of mourning that the sages did not want it performed on *Tisha B'av* for fear that the sight of the torn garment would cause a feeling of despair and depression that would be impossible to overcome. Although the first half of *Tisha B'av* is solely concerned with mourning and sadness, the second part of the day is focused on supplication, repentance, and hope.

Another answer that I heard from a student of mine is as follows. There is a fundamental difference between the mourning for a person and the mourning over the destruction. A person is helpless when faced with the death of a loved one. Man cannot control death. Man can only react to it, and he does so by tearing his garment as a sign of total frustration and helplessness. The destruction of the Temple was caused by Man's sins and therefore, the Talmud teaches that Man has the ability to rebuild the Temple by repenting for those sins. Since the Second Temple was destroyed because of the sin of "*Sinat Chinam* - Baseless Hatred", Man can repent and rebuild the Temple by loving and caring for his fellow Man. Therefore, unlike the frustration that causes the tearing after someone dies, the sorrow caused by the destruction is not irreversible. Man has the power to take control of his actions and change them in a way that will allow the rebuilding of the Temple. *Kriyah* - Tearing is not required on *Tisha B'av*, for it is a day that requires just the opposite: mending. When we are able to unite as one harmonious and loving family we will surely see the rebuilding of the Temple, may it happen very soon.

Tisha B'av - *Is Anything Wrong?*

A great rabbi who was a student of the Baal Shem Tov, the founder of the Chassidic movement, decided to journey to the Land of Israel. Before leaving on this arduous journey he went to visit his teacher to ask for a blessing. The Baal Shem Tov blessed him, but added one caveat. He told his student to be careful to answer any questions he might be asked with absolute honesty. The student found the warning somewhat strange and even slightly insulting, but was nevertheless thankful for the blessing and set off on his journey.

Several weeks later the ship that was taking the rabbi across the Mediterranean was forced to set aground on a deserted island for emergency repairs. As the day was Friday and *Shabbat* was quickly approaching the rabbi had no idea how he would possibly be able to observe the holy day. Suddenly, an old man with a long white beard emerged from the forest and invited the rabbi to spend *Shabbat* with him in his hut near the beach. The rabbi was so shocked and grateful by the old man's sudden appearance that he didn't press him with questions about how he lived on this island, and just enjoyed a wonderful *Shabbat* with the old Jew.

When *Shabbat* was over the old man escorted the rabbi back to the ship, which was repaired and ready to sail. As he wished the rabbi a safe journey the old man asked, "It's been so long since I had any contact with Jews. How are the Children of Abraham faring in the exile?" The rabbi answered, "Baruch Hashem, thank God we are surviving." The men parted and the rabbi continued his journey.

After spending time in the Holy Land the rabbi returned to Poland and went to visit the Baal Shem Tov. The Baal Shem refused to see him. The rabbi continued waiting for several days, pleading for an audience with the master. Finally he was allowed to enter. The man burst into tears and begged his master to tell him what he had wrong to deserve the master's anger. The Baal Shem Tov then reminded the rabbi of his warning to answer any question with complete honesty. "Did you meet an old man on an island in the course of your journey?" The rabbi, shocked that his master knew of the encounter, nodded. "Why did you not answer him honestly?" The rabbi didn't understand, so the Baal Shem continued. "That old man who asked for the welfare of the children of Abraham was actually our patriarch Abraham. Had you told him the truth, that we suffer tremendously in the lands of our exile and are persecuted mercilessly by our enemies, he would have cried out to God and forced Him to send the Messiah immediately."

Reflections

The real tragedy of Tisha B'av today is that we don't even realize that there's anything really wrong with our situation. We live safe, comfortable lives in the greatest democratic society in the world with the absolute freedom to observe our religion any way we please. The enormous assimilation rate and spiritual emptiness that surrounds us and effects us in ways we might not even be aware of doesn't seem to bother us. Boruch Hashem, everything is just fine. The first step towards redemption is realizing that we are in need of it.

In order to repair the damage of Tisha B'av and bring the final redemption we first must recognize and admit that we need to be redeemed. We can only do this by learning about our heritage and religion and by becoming active and involved Jews. The more involved we become the more we will realize how much further we need to go. Then we will understand the meaning of Tisha B'av, and only then will God send us the final redemption that we so desperately need.

NACHAMU – *Consolation*

T h e *Shabbat* directly following the fast of *Tisha B'av* is called *Nachamu*, "be consoled". The name is taken from the prophet Isaiah who prophesized the return of the Jewish people from their exile to Israel. The prophecy begins with the words, "*Nachamu, Nachamu*".

Whenever there is, what seems to be, a superfluous word in the *Torah* the Rabbis make every effort to derive meaning from it. What is the meaning of the repetition of *Nachamu*, be consoled?

The simple answer is that the word is repeated for dramatic effect. The *Torah* often uses the language of common speech and repeating a word or phrase in Hebrew is a common way of emphasizing a point.

Another answer is textual in nature. A few lines further in the prophecy Isaiah says that Jerusalem has received a double punishment from God. Therefore, it would follow that a double measure of consolation would also be required, as expressed by the repetition of "*Nachamu*".

There is, I think, a deeper answer. The act of consolation is usually an attempt to convince the person suffering the loss that their situation is not as hopeless as they think and that they will persevere and move forward with their lives. While a person is encouraged to perpetuate the memory of a deceased relative, they are simultaneously encouraged to "move on" with life. A person who experiences a break up or divorce is obligated to continue searching for their true partner.

This understanding of consolation doesn't seem to apply to the tragedy of the destruction of the Temple and the exile of the Jews. Can we move on and lead totally normal lives in exile without our Temple? The answer is clearly no. A large portion of the *Torah* can only be fulfilled in Israel, with a functioning Temple. We remember and mourn our loss every day in our prayers and in many of our customs. In fact, we are forbidden from forgetting the destruction and the exile. Where then is the consolation that we read about – *Nachamu, Nachamu*?

The answer is that there are two types of consolation, a temporary one and a permanent one. The temporary consolation is there to get us through the day. In a way, it is a bit of an illusion, a dream. This is the meaning of the verse that we read in the *Shir Hamaalot* before benching, "when God returns the captives of Zion it will be as if we were dreaming". The only way we can get through this long exile is by being able to dream, to look at the world through the fog of illusion. We know that we are still in exile, yet we act as if we are free.

Permanent consolation can only come with the return of all the Jews to Israel and rebuilding of the Temple. This is the *Nachamu* that Isaiah speaks of. Until that time, which should come speedily in our days, we must be content with the first *Nachamu* to get us through the darkness and confusion of exile on a national and on a personal level.

Is there a way for us to achieve the second, and complete, *Nachamu* through our actions? The prophet continues in the *Haftarah* to give us the formula for bringing that final consolation (Isaiah 40:1-5).

> "A voice calls out: Clear a way for God in the wilderness. Level a highway in the desert for God. Every valley will be raised, and every mountain and hill will be lowered. The crooked will be made level, and the ridges will become a plain. God's Glory will be revealed and all flesh will see it, for God has spoken."

The answer, according to Isaiah's prophecy, is to connect to God by recognizing his presence in every aspect of the world. God's presence in the world is evident to those who are willing and able to open their eyes and see. Every birth, sunrise, tornado, Tsunami, and rainbow is a Divine display. The only way we can actually "see" God is to first remove all of the obstacles, the mountains and valleys, that cloud, blur, and obstruct our vision. Once we have built a clear highway to God, He will no longer be hidden to us. The appearance that God is hidden or absent, *Hester Panim*, is the cause of all evil in the world. When God's presence is fully revealed there is no room for sin or evil, for no person can dare sin in the presence of His overwhelming Glory.

May we all merit to bring the redemption and to take part in the final consolation together in our Holy Temple in Jerusalem.

Tu B'Av – *The Circle*

The Talmud teaches that the two happiest days in the Jewish calendar are Yom Kippur and the fifteenth of Av (*Tu B'Av*), for on those days the single woman of Jerusalem would go out into the vineyards wearing borrowed (so as not to embarrass the poorer girls) white dresses and call out to the young men, "lift up your eyes and see what you are choosing.   Don't look at outer beauty but rather look for a good upbringing and family." *Tu B'Av*, then, is the ultimate Jewish singles event!

At the end of the chapter relating to *Tu B'Av* the Talmud recounts a story. In the future God will gather all of the righteous in a circle and will sit in the middle of them in the Garden of Eden. All the righteous will then point at God and say, "this is the God that we have trusted in and who has saved us". This is obviously a very deep message with hidden meanings, but why is it connected to *Tu B'Av*?

Tu B'Av is the fifteenth day in Av. In the Hebrew *Tu B'Av* can also be read as "the fifteenth letter in the *Alef Bet*" (Av is *Alef Bet*, the Hebrew alphabet). The fifteenth letter of the Alef Bet is *Samech*. The letter *Samech* is written as a circle. A circle represents completion. It also represents a continuum. The Jewish calendar can be viewed as a circle with points marking specific spiritual energies. For example, *Pesach* has the energy of freedom, *Sukkot* - trust in God, and *Chanukah* – miracles. As we go through the cycle of the year we experience these energies anew every time.   To further bolster this idea of cycle the Jewish year begins with the energy of *Teshuva*, which means Returning. We start the year by returning to the beginning of the cycle.

The one important thing about this cycle is that we are obligated to use the energies of the year to learn and grow. When we begin the cycle anew we should be doing so having reached new heights of growth and awareness from the previous cycle. History is also a cycle. It repeats itself constantly. Those who learn from the past avoid its mistakes but those who view it as linear and never look back fall blindly into its traps.

Tu B'av is the last holiday in the yearly cycle. It is the last point in the circle and therefore is the point from which we can look back at the entire cycle passed. It also directly follows the most tragic period of Jewish history and is therefore the perfect vantage point for looking back at our history. As we look back at our year and our history we need to search for God in the events that have transpired. Often it is only through hindsight that we can recognize the hand of God. If we search for God in everything that happens in our lives and in the world we will merit to be among those righteous who sit in the circle and can actually point to God and say, "oh yes, now I see God so clearly in every part of this circle of life."

SHABBAT - *The Third Meal*

There is a *Mitzvah* to have three meals on *Shabbat*, on Friday night, *Shabbat* morning, and *Shabbat* afternoon after *Mincha*. The first two meals begin with Kiddush over wine and challah and are replete with traditional *Shabbat* delicacies. The third meal, however, is different. There is no Kiddush recited over the third meal nor is there any tradition of eating a large meal. Instead, the third *Shabbat* meal usually just consists of some challah and a small amount of fish, salad, fruit or cake. Why isn't the third meal accorded the same stature and importance as the first two *Shabbat* meals?

The *Torah* tells us that, during their journeys through the wilderness, the Jewish people were directed and protected by the clouds of glory during the day, and by a pillar of fire at night. By observing and following these devices the people knew when to journey and when to rest, and in what direction to travel.

There is a period of time in Jewish law called *"Beyn Hashmashot"*, which literally translated means "between the suns", and refers to the time between sunset and nightfall. This time period is commonly referred to as twilight. In Jewish law there are *Mitzvot* that can only be performed by day and there are those that must be performed at night. Twilight always presents a problem because it is neither day nor night, and therefore, there is always a *"safek"*, or uncertainty, regarding the performance of these *Mitzvot* during that time. Based on this, when the Jews were in the wilderness, what protected and led them during *"Beyn Hashmashot"*? Was it the daytime clouds or the nighttime fire?

The commentaries do not address this question, so there is no way for us to know for certain. The technical answer is that since God knows exactly when day ends and night begins, there was no *"safek"* at all. There is also, however, a homiletical way of answering the question that teaches us a powerful lesson.

The Jews followed the clouds and fire without question. God wanted to give them a time when they would be forced to use their own thinking and judgment to make choices. This time was *"Beyn Hashmashot"*, when there were neither clouds nor fire leading them. During this brief time period the Jews had to think for themselves and make decisions based on their own understanding of God and *Torah*.

The third meal of *Shabbat* takes place during "*Beyn Hashmashot*" because it is a time for every person to think for themselves about their lives and the direction they are moving in. That's why food is not the focus of the meal, because food is nourishment for the body, but the third meal is a time for nourishing the mind and the soul. The third meal is a time for connecting with God, our soul, and the entire Jewish nation.

In light of this it is clear why the Rabbis refer to the third meal as being a taste of the World to Come.

SHABBAT AND MISHKAN

There are thirty nine creative activities that are prohibited on *Shabbat* by *Torah* law. These acts, *melachot*, are derived, in the Talmud, from the tasks required to construct the *Mishkan* in the desert. What is the connection between *Shabbat* and the *Mishkan* that compelled the Sages to derive the laws for one from the other?

The ultimate form of praise is imitation. We praise God and grow closer to Him by emulating His attributes and actions. For example, the Talmud teaches that "just as God is merciful so too should you be merciful" and continues by giving other examples of this. By observing *Shabbat* we emulate God's having "rested" from the creation of the world. Just as the world was God's first creation and it was holy, so too was the *Mishkan* our first holy creation. Therefore, when we "rest" on *Shabbat*, we emulate God by resting from the particular tasks that we used to create our own world of holiness, the *Mishkan*.

ROSH CHODESH – *God following Man*

According to the Talmud the first commandment that was given to the Jewish people as a nation was the *Mitzvah* of proclaiming the new month. The Jewish calendar follows the lunar cycle on a monthly basis and the solar calendar on a yearly or seasonal basis. Therefore, the appearance of the new moon marks the beginning of the new month. When the Sanhedrin resided on the Temple Mount in Jerusalem the procedure for proclaiming the new month was as follows. Two witnesses would testify before the court that they had seen the new moon. After confirming their, testimony the court would proclaim either that day or the following day as the first of the month. They would immediately send messengers to the Diaspora informing all of the dispersed communities of their proclamation. It took the messengers in some cases over two weeks to reach all of the Diaspora communities. When the holidays of Succot and Pesach arrived on the fifteenth day of their respective months those communities who had not yet heard the decision of the Jerusalem court could not be certain which day was actually the fifteenth. In order not to mistakenly violate the actual holiday, these communities would observe an additional day to be certain. Although the calendar was calculated and fixed after the destruction of the Temple, this custom of observing two days of holiday in the Diaspora continues up until today.

Why was this *Mitzvah* chosen as the first to be presented to the nation of Israel? The *Mitzvah* of proclaiming the new moon is unique in that it gives the Jewish People the power to determine the exact time of the holidays. By doing so it also gives them the power over all of the *Mitzvot* relating to those days. For example, the *Torah* punishes anyone who consumes bread on Pesach. When does that punishment actually take effect? That depends on when the court declared the new moon. If the court determines that Pesach should fall out on a Monday then God follows that ruling and punishes the perpetrator who transgresses on Monday. The example of Yom Kippur is even stronger. The *Torah* calls Yom Kippur the unique day when God grants the Jews atonement for their sins. When exactly that day falls is entirely determined by the Jewish court. What flows from this is that the Jews tell God on what day to forgive them, and He listens!

As part of the *Torah* given at Sinai, God gave the Jewish People the ability to develop laws which He then accepts as His own. This idea is really the basis for Rabbinic Judaism. As long as they work within the strict parameters of the Oral Tradition received at Sinai, the Sages have the power to interpret the *Torah*, and those interpretations and laws are then accepted by God as *Torah*.

This is why the first *Mitzvah* given to the Jews was the New Moon. It sets the basis and foundation for the understanding and interpretation of the Oral Law as received at Sinai and developed throughout history.

Reflections

This is an example of God allowing Man to be His partner. Other examples include circumcision and *Tzedakah*. God could have caused Man to be born circumcised, yet he allowed Man to make himself complete. God could sustain the poor, yet he gave Man the opportunity to do it as His agent. It's a great honor to be partners with God.

Sermons

2004 - 2007

CHUKAT – *Moses, You're Fired*

Imagine that Donald Trump calls you and asks you to be the CEO of one of his development companies. Your job will be to build a magnificent fifty story skyscraper in NYC. The project will take five years. There's one catch. Donald tells you that during each of the five years you will only be paid a token salary, just enough to cover living expenses, but everyone will think that you are getting paid a huge salary. However, after the five years and the project are completed, you will receive 100 million dollars. You are cautious and a bit insecure, but you figure that you can sweat out those five years and then take home more money than you or your offspring for several generations to come will ever be able to spend, so you take the job.

The job is tough. You are under constant pressure to complete everything according to Trump's exacting specifications. You are under the constant scrutiny of the shareholders, the government, the IRS, FBI, SEC, the labor unions, and the press. You have absolutely no privacy and basically no family life.

Despite the impossible conditions you perform well. You introduce innovative techniques to improve the building quality. You motivate your labor force to produce stellar results in record time. You withstand all public scrutiny and emerge unscathed. Finally, you complete the skyscraper on time and under budget in exactly five years.

Now you await your reward. After five years of financial struggle and material depravation you can finally see the light at the end of the tunnel. You have earned the 100 million dollars promised to you. At the grand opening of the skyscraper, and your payday, you are called upon to introduce Donald Trump to address the thousands of spectators gathered, and the millions of TV viewers tuned in, to witness the event. In your excitement you've forgotten the index card listing all of the Donald's companies and achievements so you just "wing it" by saying, "and now presenting the man that needs no introduction...Donald Trump". Trump shoots you an angry look before beginning his speech.

After the event Trump calls you up to his boardroom. You enter the room expecting to receive your long awaited pay check. Instead Trump says, "you've done a great job in getting my project completed on time and under budget. However, you had the chance to really show your thanks and to honor me in front of the entire world by introducing me in the manner that I deserve, by enumerating my great achievements and accomplishments. Instead, you disrespected me by not saying anything. Unfortunately, by disrespecting me you nullified all the great work you did for me and you also nullified our deal. Not only will I not pay you the 100 million dollars but...you're fired. You are devastated. All the work, sacrifice and hardship that you willingly endured just to get that final reward. All gone.

This is the story of Moses and his final punishment of not being allowed to enter the Land of Israel. God first contacts Moses when he is just a shepherd, and asks him to lead the Jewish People out of Egypt. His only reward will be the honor and privilege of entering the land of Israel. Moses at first rejects the offer out of insecurity and humbleness, but after some effective persuasion by God, reluctantly accepts.

For the next forty years Moses successfully leads the Jewish People. He splits the Sea of Reeds, brings down the *Torah* at Mount Sinai, guides, teaches, counsels, and provides for millions of people in the wilderness. Throughout this time he is constantly under the scrutiny of his people and is regularly accused of misleading them and even stealing from them. He survives a rebellion and several minor disturbances while doing only the best for the people with no thought to his own well being or honor. He is even forced to sacrifice his family life to always be prepared to receive prophecy directly from God.

After nearly forty years of total self sacrifice to his "job", Moses eagerly anticipates his reward, the land of Israel. When the people cry for water God tells him to take his staff and speak to the rock. Moses somehow misunderstands God's exact instructions and instead of just speaking to the rock, he also hits it with his staff and, miraculously, enough water gushes from the rock to sustain the entire nation. Afterwards God tells Moses that because he didn't follow his exact instruction to speak to the rock and thereby missed an opportunity to glorify God's Name before the people, he would be punished by not being allowed to enter Israel.

Moses' lifelong hope and dream, destroyed because of a seemingly minor misstep? How can this severe punishment be a fair match for the "crime" committed?

The truth is that if an ordinary person would have hit the rock he probably would only have gotten a slight reprimand. Moses, the greatest prophet and leader to ever grace the world, should have known better than to ignore God's instructions to achieve the desired result, and was therefore held to a much higher standard. In this case the positive end did not justify the means.

A more modern example is Bill Clinton. He committed a sin during his presidency that is commonplace throughout modern society and is often either ignored or even sometimes envied and idolized. If he had been just an ordinary citizen he would have moved on with his life without much fanfare. As president of the United States, however, Bill Clinton was held to a much higher standard and was publicly humiliated and nearly impeached.

Like Moses, Jews today are also held to a higher standard. For example, when US military forces mistakenly inflict civilian casualties during necessary urban combat the casualties are classified as collateral damage and the military is rightfully excused. When the Israel Defense Force enters urban areas (e.g. Jenin) to destroy terrorist cells and risks Israeli lives to avoid hurting civilians but unwillingly inflicts civilian casualties because the terrorists are shooting from among the civilian population, the IDF is accused of war crimes and massacres. Although this primarily stems from anti-semitism, it also reflects the belief that Jews should exhibit a higher degree of morality.

The Jewish people are held to a higher standard by the world, and every Jew is judged as a representative of the entire Jewish people. This sounds like a daunting responsibility for every Jew to bear. There is an easy way out of this situation. We can just stop being Jewish. But is that really an option for us? Should we then avoid everything that is meaningful if it requires hard work and sacrifice? If every person who thought about being a doctor decided to give up their dream because of the hard work and sacrifice required to achieve it we would have no doctors. The same is true for any meaningful vocation or achievement. If we feel that Judaism has meaning and is important to us then we must invest the work and self sacrifice required to make it a part of our lives. We cannot just give it up.

There is, then, only one option left. We must accept the responsibility of representing Judaism and the Jewish people and bear that responsibility with pride and dignity by living our lives to the highest standards of morality as taught in our *Torah*. We must fulfill our destiny to be "a light unto the nations". Since we are judged by higher standards we must make every effort to live by those higher standards. By doing so, we will bring honor to the entire Jewish people and glory to the Name of God.

KORACH - *Making Sense of Judaism*

There is a *Mitzvah* to affix a Mezuzah, consisting of the first two paragraphs of the Shema written on a small piece of parchment, to the doorpost of every room in a Jewish home. The mezuzah commemorates the blood that the Jews smeared on their doorposts to serve as a sign for God to protect them from the final plague in Egypt. The Mezuzah signifies protection of the home. Question. What if you have a house filled with *Torah* scrolls? Would it still require a mezuzah that contains only a tiny portion of a single *Torah,* or would the presence of the *Torah*s be sufficient to fulfill the commandment and protect the house?

There's a *Mitzvah* for men to wear *Tzizit,* strings that are attached to the four corners of a special garment. The *Tzizit* are supposed to be white except for one string which must be "T'chaylet", a unique bluish dye obtained from a rare snail. This blue color is supposed to remind us of the sky, which in turn is associated with heaven and God. What if the entire garment is blue? Is the single blue string still required?

According to the *Midrash* these two cases, the Mezuzah and the *Tzizit,* formed the basis for the rebellion of Korach, a Levite prince who tried to replace Moses and Aaron as leaders of the nation. Therefore, in order to understand what exactly this rebellion was about we need to first understand the underlying arguments behind these two cases. There are two distinct lines of reasoning within these arguments.

The first line of reasoning is purely logical. A Mezuzah contains a parchment with the first two paragraphs of the Shema written on it. A *Torah* scroll contains those two paragraphs and much more. Therefore, logic would dictate that a room full of *Torah* scrolls would not require a Mezuzah. This same line of logical reasoning would also apply to the *Tzizit* case.

The second line of reasoning goes beyond logic and addresses one of the most challenging issues relating to religious observance. Getting back to the *Mitzvah* of *Tzizit,* the blue "*T'chaylet*" string is supposed to direct our thoughts to the image of heaven. What if I have another way of inspiring my thoughts to reach the same goal as the string? What if I wear a blue shirt? What if, to remember that God created the world in six days and rested on the seventh, I sit around a camp fire on *Shabbat* and burn incense and write poetry? What if instead of getting married under a *chupah* with a ring, a ketubah, and the proper blessings, I decide to marry my beloved by way of a bungee jump?

Let's move away from the realm of religion and into an area which we are all more familiar with. Let's say you're dating or married, and its birthday time. As a man I find this to be an extremely challenging event. Besides the ordeal of choosing an appropriate gift I'm thinking, "What's the big deal about the day of birth anyway?" Now, just imagine this scenario. It's the day after the birthday and I meet up with my beloved. She doesn't seem very happy...no, she's fuming! How could you forget my birthday!!

But wait...am I fazed? Absolutely not! I look at her with the sweetest and most innocent smile and say, "Sweetheart, I most definitely remembered your birthday. How could I forget? Yesterday I went, with my guitar, to the very same bench in the park where we first met and I played your favorite song and thought about you all afternoon. I felt so close to you, and so much love and appreciation that you are in my life. Happy birthday." See any problem with my gift?

There are specific feelings attached to specific actions. Giving someone a gift on their birthday is more meaningful than giving it to them the day after. There is an etiquette that defines and directs our actions. When we meet someone we shake their hand. We don't slap their cheek, kiss their forehead, or step on their big toe. Even though we might feel that these unique ways of greeting show our affection and respect for the person, we realize that generally accepted etiquette says differently.

God gave the Jewish People rules and etiquette to follow to get close to Him. We don't always understand the meaning behind all of these rules and some of the etiquettes are strange and illogical, but we trust and believe that they are true and divine and through them we will be able to reach our full spiritual potential and fulfill our ultimate destiny as individuals and as a nation.

Furthermore, every *Mitzvah* has a mystical component to it that causes a spiritual reaction and generates spiritual energies that affect the universe and propel us closer to God. When we light candles before *Shabbat* we are not only lighting up our dinning rooms but we are bringing holiness, light, and peace into the entire world. When we say a blessing over the wine and the challah, we are blessing the world with sustenance and bounty, and releasing the spiritual energy that brings peace of mind and satisfaction to every human being. Every action that we take, every *Mitzvah* that we perform, literally changes the world and brings humanity closer to God.

Korach wanted to circumvent the *Mitzvot* and find spirituality through his own logic and thought process. This was viewed as a rebellion against God. However, was Korach completely wrong in his thinking? Is there no place for individual feeling and emotion in the performance of the *Mitzvot*?

Every person needs to find his own unique way of experiencing the *Mitzvot* based on his own talents, interests, and character. At the beginning of the Amidah we say, "God of Abraham, God of Isaac, and God of Jacob". Why doesn't it just say, "God of Abraham, Isaac, and Jacob"? The Shelah Hakadosh, a great seventeenth century Kabbalist in Jerusalem explained, that each of the Patriarchs had his own unique relationship with God based on his unique strengths. Abraham served God mainly through the attribute of *Chesed*, Isaac through Awe, and Jacob through Truth. We each need to find our own unique "style" in serving God.

For example, when we recite the ancient and holy words of the *Siddur*, the prayer book, are we just doing so in a rote and dry manner or are we looking into the deeper meanings of the prayers and making them our own? Are we singing and dancing through them or are we simply rushing through to finish them as quickly as possible? Is our *Shabbat* filled with singing, learning, and connecting with friends or family or is it just a maze of restrictions and boredom to be endured until *Havdalah* and the movie theatre on Saturday night?

Judaism requires both the technical, and often illogical, performance of the *Mitzvot* AND the emotional and "Spiritual" feelings that touch our individual souls. The resulting combination will bring us closer to God, true spirituality, and the fulfillment of our destinies.

RE'EH – *Seeing is Believing*

This week's *Parsha* begins in a unique way, with Moses telling the Jewish People to "Re'eh - see" the blessings and the curses that will be given to them. Firstly, you can't "see" a blessing or a curse being given. Secondly, these blessings and curses referred to by Moses would only be given on Mount Gerizim and Mount Abel in the Land of Israel, years later. So what is there to see now? It should say "Hear". In fact, "hear" is used quite often in the *Torah*. The most famous example is the Shema. "Hear Israel, Hashem is your God, Hashem is One." Maybe it should have said, "See Israel"? To answer this question, we need to first examine and define the practical difference between hearing and seeing.

What happens when you hear? A sound comes into contact with the ear. You first need to identify it. Who is speaking? Is it a voice that you need to give your attention to? After identifying it you need to process the content of the message being conveyed. You might need to translate or interpret that message in order to properly understand it. Only after thoroughly processing it can you finally respond appropriately. Many people don't actually go through this process, which is why there are so many misunderstandings and problems in the world. People sometimes listen but they don't hear. Hearing is a two step process. Physically hearing the sound, and intellectually processing it. For example, the sound of the shofar is supposed to wake us up to think about improving the way we lead our lives. According to the Halacha, if you're walking down the street on Rosh Hashanah and just happen to hear the sound of the shofar without realizing what it is, you have not fulfilled your obligation. Hearing the sound is not enough. The sound must be intellectually processed to be considered valid.

Shema Yisrael. Did you ever think why we need to say, "Shema Yisrael – Hear Israel"? Why can't we just say, "Hashem is Our God, Hashem is One", the actual proclamation of faith? Based on our previous explanation, simply saying words to accept God's mastery upon us is not enough. We need to intellectually understand and process that message so that it becomes part of our very being, and not just something we give "lip service" too.

Now let's examine seeing. Seeing does not require the same degree of analysis as hearing. Identifying something or someone you see is usually immediate. Seeing does not require advanced intellectual processing. You can hear about someone stealing or cheating but you never know whether to believe it or not. One brief visual, though, and you know it's true. That's where the term comes from...seeing is believing.

I'd like to go one step further. I believe that there is a "seeing" that goes beyond the normal, physical sense. When the Jews stood at the foot of Mount Sinai to receive the *Torah* the verse says, "The whole nation *saw* the sounds and the flames, and the sound of the shofar and the smoking mountain. And the nation *saw* and trembled and stood from a distance." What does it mean to see the sound? There are two explanations in the Talmud. One is that they were actually given the super human ability to see sound waves. The other is that their normal vision remained unchanged. However, the barriers clouding their vision and preventing them from seeing were removed in that instance, allowing them to see the supernatural.

We all see things through the barriers that we ourselves often create. Therefore, we see things from our own perspective. We all have preconceived notions about people that we meet and, based on those, we form opinions and make judgments regarding them. This is how we navigate through life, seeing things as we perceive them based on our personal perspectives and feelings.

Then, something changes and we are hit with a flash of realization. Clarity. Suddenly, everything looks different and makes perfect sense. I like to call it "soul seeing" because it has nothing to do with the intellect. It is beyond the intellect. These moments of clarity change people lives. Often these moments come as a result of death or tragedy. After the 9/11 disaster thousands reevaluated their career and life goals and made drastic changes in their lives. But these moments of clarity also come in good times. The decision to marry comes in that moment of clarity.

The vision that the Jews at Sinai experienced was beyond the normal "seeing". Their "seeing" was one of total and complete clarity. Their faith at that moment was clear and absolute. This is what Moses, in this week's *Parsha*, is telling the Jewish People, "Re'eh – See". Look beyond your preconceived notions and your ingrained prejudices and let your soul see with the pure clarity that only it can do. Only then will you truly be able to comprehend the blessings of God.

A great example of this concept is *Shabbat*. On *Shabbat* the barriers of the six days of creation that often interfere with our attempts to connect with the spiritual are removed. There is complete "rest" or silence allowing us to "see" and experience the spiritual and Divine obstructed from our vision during the rest of the week.

The month of Elul begins the thirty day countdown to Rosh Hashanah during which time we reevaluate our lives and try to improve. It's hard to make those changes when our eyes are covered with blinders, preventing us from seeing our true selves. Re'eh. See. Take off those blockers and see the world with fresh, new clarity. Then make the necessary changes and improvements, and grow in ways you never thought possible.

Re'eh. All you need to do is to "see".

Kɪ Teytzey – *War, Captives, Teshuvah*

This week's *Parsha* of *Ki Teytze* begins with an unusual law that is extremely uncomfortable and objectionable to the modern Western mind. I'd like to examine this law and offer two different interpretations that will, I hope, not only help us understand it on a literal level, but also give us new and important insights into ourselves and the process of repentance.

The *Parsha* begins with the verse, "When you will go out to war against your enemy, and God will give him to you in victory and you will take prisoners". The *Torah* then goes on to describe a very unusual law. If, while in battle, a Jewish soldier captures a woman that he desires he may take her as a wife as long as she leaves behind her idolatrous beliefs and converts to Judaism. Before being allowed to marry this captive the soldier must let her mourn her parents by allowing her to shave her head, wear sackcloth, and generally neglect her appearance for a period of thirty days. Only then, if he stills desires her, does the *Torah* permit them to wed.

Our initial reaction is, "How can the *Torah* permit this? It's sinful!" The Talmud answers that the *Torah* is acknowledging and accepting Man's evil inclination. Since the soldier may be overcome by his desire and commit a sin, the *Torah* offers him a way of expressing his desires within its legal framework.

Is this a satisfying answer? Based on this reasoning if a man has an insatiable craving for lobster, the *Torah* should permit him to eat it, maybe just once. Man's evil inclination is constantly on the lookout for ways to fulfill the desires of his heart, but the *Torah* implores us to conquer those desires that go against its' teachings. Why then does the *Torah* surrender to the Evil Inclination in the case of the *Yifat Toar* – Female Captive?

To answer this question we need to examine the context within which this law arises: War. War presents possibly the greatest enigma to the religious thinker. The most precious thing in the world is human life. The world was created for Man, and only he has the ability to make it holy and meaningful by his actions. Without Man, the world has no purpose.

The greatest tragedy therefore is death, and the most heinous sin is murder. The *Torah* teaches that if someone holds a gun to your head and tells you to kill someone or be killed, you must give up your life rather than murder another. The same *Torah*, however, also commands us to make war, either to conquer the land of Israel, in self defense, or even to attain certain economic or political objectives. In war, the terrible sin of murder suddenly becomes a *Mitzvah*! Our greatest moral guidelines and teachings are overturned and discarded, and our basest instincts are given free reign to run wild. The Jewish soldier goes to battle under strict orders from his greatest religious leaders and teachers to kill and destroy the enemy in any way possible, without mercy, knowing that if he fails, his family and homeland will be wiped out. There is no room for compassion, sensitivity, or kindness. His thoughts must be focused completely on killing.

Once the *Torah* permits the evil inclination to dominate us in the form of a *Mitzvah* it cannot expect us to, at the same time, overpower it. Therefore, its' only choice is to attempt to confine the sin and control its' consequences. This is the law of Yifat Toar.

I'd like to focus on this idea of acknowledging and accepting our evil inclination. The *Torah* is not simply a holy religious book written for saints. It is a guidebook to life written for all mankind. It addresses horrible sins such as murder, theft, and immorality, because these things do, unfortunately, occur. Man has tremendous potential for holiness and purity but also tremendous potential for the most terrible evil imaginable. The first step to growth and repentance is to acknowledge our weaknesses. Someone who loves lobster shouldn't try to convince himself that it really doesn't taste that great or is not healthy, because it's a lie and his subconscious will realize it, rebel against it, and refute it. Once his anti-lobster arguments are refuted, there is nothing stopping him from eating it. Rather, he should accept the fact that he has an overwhelming desire for the slimy creature but that he cannot partake of it, solely because the *Torah* forbids him to.

Another example of this is when we are faced with a member of the opposite sex who we desire, but cannot pursue for a reason that we accept, i.e. they're not Jewish, they're married, we're married etc. If we deny our desire, which is a lie, our minds will find a way to refute the denial arguments. If we trivialize it by saying that it's really nothing and let our guard down we run the risk of succumbing in a moment of weakness and passion. The only way to attempt to control the desire is to acknowledge that it is real.

Now that we've acknowledged our weakness and desire, how do we deal with it? The most practical, and possibly only, way is to avoid the challenging situation. Going up to Maine and touring the lobster eateries is not going to help the lobster craver in his battle. Going out for coffee at night with the object of your forbidden desire will not help you avoid succumbing. Our desires are real and, in fact, quite healthy. Thinking that we are strong enough to withstand them is foolish and just plain wrong.

But what happens if we can't always avoid our desires and temptations? What if we don't want to because those desires are for something that is very dear and important to us? Many times people who become more observant face this issue. For example, let's say a woman was a dancer or cheerleader before becoming observant. She still loves dancing but obviously cannot pursue a professional cheerleading career due to issues of religious modesty. Must she then avoid dancing completely and wipe that very special talent and desire from her heart? The law of the *Yifat Toar* holds the answer to this dilemma.

Looking beyond the literal and technical aspects of this law the Chassidic Masters explain that going out to war refers to every person's battle against their own evil inclination. When, with God's help, we are successful in our battle, we often face difficult issues regarding our past actions. The beautiful woman we so desire and hold captive is that beloved desire from our past that we don't want, or are not ready to, relinquish. The *Torah* teaches us that we don't have to discard it, but rather, we can bring it into our home and integrate it into our new life. We might have to make some minor adaptations but we can certainly continue to enjoy our beloved "captive" within the context of a *Torah* lifestyle. Talents, culture, humor, sports, and entertainment can all be successfully integrated into *Torah* living.

Although being a cheerleader might be out of the question, being a dancer in the proper venues is encouraged. The comedian who used to work blue can now tell clean jokes. Even the lobster lover can find some imitation version that might in some way satisfy him.

This message is especially relevant to the month of Elul, the pre High Holiday period during which we reflect on our lives and try to improve ourselves and our relationships. After serious reflection we should be ready to make changes in our lives in line with our goals for the upcoming New Year. These changes should complement and embrace the positive aspects of our personalities and lives instead of overwhelming and negating them.

The law of the *Yifat Toar* – Female Captive teaches us to first acknowledge our weaknesses and desires, and then decide on the appropriate way of dealing with them. We can either try to avoid them, integrate them into our *Torah* lifestyle, or a combination of the two.

May God give us the strength to face our weaknesses and desires and deal with them appropriately so that we can grow successfully as Jews and as human beings.

THE ESSENCE OF TESHUVAH

According to Jewish tradition Rosh Hashanah is the Day of Judgment. Many of the customs and laws relating to and revolving around the holiday reflect this. For example, we wear the white jacket, or *kitel*, we eat special foods that represent good omens, we ask people for forgiveness, and we generally conduct ourselves in a reflective and pensive manner.

Although some of the liturgical poems we recite as part of the prayer service relate to judgment, the prayer service as a whole does not. Most Rosh Hashanah prayer rites do not include confessions or selichot (penitential supplications), that are highlighted by the recitation of the thirteen attributes of mercy. Instead the service primarily is focused on the idea of God's kingship. On Rosh Hashanah we coronate God as king of the universe. However, if Rosh Hashanah is, in fact, the Day of Judgment shouldn't we be asking for forgiveness and confessing our sins? If our crowning of God is sufficient then why do we immediately follow the holiday with the ten days of repentance and Yom Kippur, which assumes that we were unsuccessful in gaining a favorable judgment?

During the Ten Days of Repentance, between Rosh Hashanah and Yom Kippur, we recite a verse in the selichot, taken from the *Torah* portion of *Nitzavim*, which seems to make no sense. We ask God to "circumcise our hearts". How can a heart be circumcised?

Finally, as the gates of repentance are closing at the end of the Neila service in the final moments of Yom Kippur, wouldn't it make sense for us to make one last plea for forgiveness or recite one final confession? Instead, we stop asking for forgiveness, and recite the Shema and proclaim that Hashem is our God (seven times).

The prophet in Samuel 2 chapter 25 recounts an interesting story. While on the run from King Saul, David, already secretly anointed King of Israel by Samuel, recruits an army of six hundred warriors and begins providing protection to the shepherds of the rich land owners in the Ein Gedi region of Israel. One of the beneficiaries of these services is a wealthy owner named Nahval. After providing protection for his shepherds during the grazing season, David sends messengers to Nahval's mansion to request payment in the form of food and supplies for his men. Not only does Nahval reject the messengers' requests, he does so in a very disrespectful manner, mocking David's name and reputation. When David hears Nahval's response, he is furious and orders his men to saddle their horses and attack Nahval's homestead.

Meanwhile, back at the ranch, Nahval's wife Avigail hears of what Nahval has done and quickly surmises the inevitable consequences of her husband's foolishness. She orders her servants to gather together the supplies that David requested and heads out to catch David and his army.

Avigail cuts David off at the pass, presents him with the supplies, and pleads for the life of her husband. David is so touched by Avigail's loyalty to her husband that he relents and turns his army back to base.

Avigail then begins her journey home, furious at her husband's stupidity and anxious to give him a rebuking that he will never forget. As she approaches the mansion she hears the sounds of partying. Nahval is having a huge party! Avigail can hardly contain her anger. Her only thought is to storm into the party and berate her husband in front of his guests. She doesn't. Instead, she just stands quietly on the side.

As the prophet describes so beautifully, the next morning, when the wine had left Nahval and he was undoubtedly reeling from a grand hangover, Avigail finally approached him and told him what he had done and how he had nearly caused his own destruction. At that moment, as the words penetrated into his very soul, his heart "turned to stone" and he remained comatose for ten days. After these ten days he died.

Why didn't Avigail berate Nahval immediately upon entering the house and finding him engaged in the party? According to Rav J.B. Soloveitchik, when someone is having a party, they cannot and will not listen to rebuke. He goes on to say that there is an Avigail following every sinner just waiting for the right moment, the end of the party, to offer rebuke.

Every person is having a party. Having a party doesn't have to refer to an actual party with food and music. It is anything that preoccupies us to such a degree that we are unable to focus on the things that really matter, be it God, *Torah*, family, relationships, or personal growth. The party could be work, school, or entertainment. While we're involved in our party, we cannot hear Avigail speaking to us. We first need to lower the volume and take a "time out" from the party before we can hear and internalize the words of our own Avigail, admonishing us to do the right thing, make the right choices, and change our ways for the better.

In order to answer our original question we need to understand the essence of Teshuvah, repentance. To do that we need to examine what exactly is a sin. If there was a police officer next to us twenty four hours every day, we would never dare to break the law. On a more positive note, if someone told us that they would write us a check for a million dollars (or even a thousand) every time we performed a *Mitzvah* I have no doubt that we would be extremely careful and diligent in performing them. If we truly believed that God was a part of our lives, standing beside us through the good and the bad times, we would find it almost impossible to "sin". We would never spread rumors or gossip. We would never embarrass anyone. We would always treat our parents with the utmost respect and honor. When we sin we are, in a way, excluding God from our lives. The great Rebbe of Kotzk once asked his students, "Where can God be found?" He answered, "Wherever you let Him in." When we sin we are in effect closing the door to keep God out of our lives. What, then, is the Teshuvah for locking God out of our lives, or sinning? It is accepting God wholeheartedly as king and master, and making Him an integral partner in every aspect of our lives.

On Rosh Hashanah we accept God as King and Master. We proclaim that this year we will take God with us when we go to work and deal with our coworkers, when we go home and interact with our parents, and when we get together and socialize with our friends. This is the essence of Teshuvah. Therefore, on the Day of Judgment our main activity is, in fact, Teshuvah. The only problem is that we're still all engaged in our parties. We are still mired beneath layers of distractions and preoccupations that prevent us from hearing the voice of Avigail admonishing us to do Teshuvah. As long as we're having our parties our Teshuvah is not complete and effective. Therefore we need the Ten Days of Repentance during which we recite Selichot to slowly bring us out of our parties by tearing away the layers of obstructions that are preventing our souls from reaching their natural and instinctive heights. We therefore ask God to "circumcise our hearts", which means to cut away those layers of obstructions preventing us from true Teshuvah.

We then spend the day of Yom Kippur fasting and begging for forgiveness. At Neila, moments before the conclusion of Yom Kippur, there is not a single Jew who is still having a party. The obstructions have been torn away. We are finally ready to do Teshuvah. Therefore, our final words on Yom Kippur, just as the Gates of Repentance are closing, are the Shema and "Hashem is Our God". We accept God as our King and recognize that He is always with us. This is the essence of Teshuvah which we can only experience at the very end of Yom Kippur when are minds and souls are free of all "parties".

May God always be with us in our hearts and souls and bless each of us and our loved ones with health, love, success, peace and the strength and desire to grow as Jews and as human beings in this new year.

Succot – *The Framwork of Life*

The *Midrash* teaches that when the Messiah comes and the entire world recognizes the Divine plan and accepts the Oneness of God, the world will see the rewards, either spiritual or material, enjoyed by the Jewish People, and complain. They will claim that had they been given the opportunity to perform the *Mitzvot,* they too would receive those same rewards. In response, God will offer them the opportunity to perform one *Mitzvah* which, if they succeed, will entitle them to the same rewards as the Jewish People. That *Mitzvah* will be the Succah. Satisfied with the terms of the offer, the non Jews proceed to build a Succah and to dwell in it. However, God removes the sun's protective covering allowing it to shine with such intense force upon the land that the non Jews, unable to withstand the heat, kick the Succah and return to their homes. By doing so, they give up their chance to share in the rewards of the Messianic age.

According to Halacha, severe discomfort is valid grounds for leaving the Succah. Therefore, since the non Jews left the Succah because of the extraordinarily intense heat, why are they penalized? They are not Halachically obligated to remain in the Succah under those circumstances! The answer to this question lies not in the legality of their leaving the Succah, but rather, in their manner of leaving. Whereas when Jews leave a Succah because of unbearable conditions they do so reluctantly, with a heavy heart, the non Jews in the *Midrash* kick the Succah with disdain on their way out.

There is a deeper question regarding this *Midrash*. Why, out of all the *Mitzvot,* is Succah chosen as the one to determine whether the world is worthy of Divine grace? Why not *Shabbat*, Yom Kippur, *Kashrut*, or any of the other fundamental precepts of Judaism?

Jewish Law is very strict in dictating the specific materials permitted for use as *Schach*, the covering of the Succah. Firstly, the material must have grown from the ground. For example, plastic rods are not permissible. Secondly, the material must be detached from the ground. Therefore, the branches of a tree attached to the ground cannot be used as *Schach* until they are cut from the tree. Thirdly, the material must not be capable of becoming Tameh, ritually impure. Therefore, any item used as a utensil or as a functioning object, such as furniture, cannot be used as *Schach*. Regarding the walls of the Succah, however, there are no restrictions. All materials are permissible. Why are there strict regulations for the *Schach* and none regarding the walls? Furthermore, the entire holiday is named after the Schach, which highlights its disproportionate importance.

Finally, in our prayers we refer to God as the One who "spreads his Succah of Peace upon us and the entire nation of Israel, and upon Jerusalem." How does one "spread" a Succah?

There is a Kabbalistic concept that everything in the physical world has an exact counterpart or duplicate image in the spiritual world, and vice versa. For example, the *Beit Hamikdash*, the Holy Temple in Jerusalem, and all its vessels and utensils were representations of different spiritual energies and forces existing in the heavenly precincts and spheres of holiness. Therefore, the destruction of that holy place represented not only a physical tragedy but also a disruption, or exile, of the Divine Presence – *Shechinah*. The Succah, I believe, represents the image of the ideal spiritual state of being, or environment, that we are truly meant to experience. According to some, this ideal spiritual existence is referred to as the Garden of Eden. According to others it is the Messianic Age. For one week we leave our material world of perceived safety and security and enter a world of simple faith and complete trust in God's grace and protection. We enter into a semblance of the way the world should ideally be.

The walls of our Succah represent the boundaries and limits that we impose on ourselves. These "walls" can take the form of careers, culture, social mores, or personal goals and objectives. Our choices of "walls" are limited only by our own decisions. God grants us the freedom to choose without restriction. The roof of our Succah, the Schach, which is regulated, represents our faith, our Judaism, which provides structure to our lives and guidelines for our actions. It allows us to pursue our dreams and fulfill our goals within the framework of its guidance and beneath the protection of its shadow. As long as we are under the Schach everything we do becomes meaningful and holy. Even the most mundane acts such as eating and drinking can become acts of holiness. Living a Jewish life means elevating and transforming the seemingly ordinary into the spiritually meaningful. It means living fulfilled every moment of the day, whether at the office, at home, or at play.

This is why the *Midrash* teaches that the *Mitzvah* of Succah was given to the world as the test of observance. The Succah doesn't represent a single *Mitzvah*. It represents the framework within which everything we do becomes holy. It is challenging and demands hard work and constant attention, but the rewards – overall fulfillment and purpose in life – are well worth the effort.

We pray that God assist us in this endeavor by spreading over us his Succah, the *Torah*, beneath and within which we can achieve fulfillment and satisfaction and transform this world into a place of love, peace and holiness.

Tisha B'av – *Eicha*

On the night of *Tisha B'av* we read the Book of Lamentations, which is named *Eicha* in Hebrew after the first word in the book. The author of the book, the prophet Jeremiah, laments the tragic destruction of Jerusalem, the Temple, and the Jewish nation.

The word *Eicha* means "how" and is used by the prophet to rhetorically ask how such a tragedy and destruction could have been allowed to occur. Based on this translation the theme of the book becomes Man's search for understanding the hidden, and often inexplicable, hand of God, and the mystery of good and evil and divine reward and punishment.

The word "*Eicha*" can also be read slightly differently to translate as "where are you", the same term addressed to Adam by God after the sin in the Garden of Eden. This usage of the word reflects a unique understanding of the tragedy of the destruction and exile. When the Temple functioned in Jerusalem the Divine Presence was clearly manifested. The prayers and offerings of the Jewish People, and the entire world, were focused towards one place. There was no doubt that God's presence dwelt amongst the Jewish People in the Holy Temple in Jerusalem.

The Talmud teaches that after the destruction the Divine Presence was exiled with the Jewish People. No longer would the glory of the *Shechinah* be openly revealed to the world. It would remain hidden as part of the punishment of exile.

The real tragedy of the exile and destruction is that we are not able to see God's presence in the world like we did when the Temple stood. In our blindness we continue to ask, "when will the Messiah finally arrive, and what can we do to speed his arrival?" The answer, however, lies clearly before our shuddered eyes. If we could just hear the word of God, the message would probably be something like this.

"I gave you back the Land of Israel and allowed you to settle there from the four corners of the world. I gave you an army and made you victorious over your enemies. I gave you Jerusalem and the Temple Mount. I made the land bloom and provided you with the means to prosper in the land. For those who remained in the exile, I placed you in a country of unparalleled freedom and democracy where you can practice Judaism without fear. I gave you synagogues, *yeshivot*, rabbis, kosher food, books in Hebrew and English, and the ability to travel to Israel in comfort. I've given you wealth and prosperity. I've done everything you asked for. Now it's your turn. All you need to do is to take advantage of these opportunities, to study *Torah*, perform the *Mitzvot*, and treat each other with love and respect."

The Rabbis teach that the Messiah can appear two different ways. If the Jews merit it, he will appear on a majestic white horse. If they don't merit it, he will appear on a ragged old donkey. Everyone recognizes a redeemer who rides a magnificent white horse. No one recognizes a redeemer on a shabby old donkey.

The Rabbis teach that *Tisha B'av* is the birthday of the Messiah, and that in each generation there is a Messiah just waiting to reveal himself. The Messiah has arrived, but we cannot recognize him. All we can see is a man on an old donkey. Despite all the signs, all we can do is ask "Eicha", "where are you?" This is the tragedy of the exile. In order to free ourselves from the exile and accept the Messianic era we must just open our eyes and take advantage of the opportunities and gifts given to us by God. We must live as Jews in every sense of the word. We must cherish the Land of Israel. Most importantly, we must embrace our brothers and sisters and unite as one family, and turn the baseless hatred that caused the destruction of the Temple into true caring and love. Only then will we merit seeing the Messiah revealed before us, and will the Fast of *Tisha B'av* be transformed into a day of rejoicing.

ISRAEL REFLECTIONS – 7/22/06

There is a teaching in the Talmud that says, "One who lives outside of the Land of Israel is as if he were an idolater." Is this statement, and others like it, to be taken literally? Are Jews outside of Israel really idolaters? Of course not. What then is the meaning behind these teachings?

One explanation offered by Rabbi Eliezer Melamed (Israel) goes as follows. The pagans believed that different Gods ruled different aspects of nature and the spirits. For example, Poseidon ruled the sea, Ra the sun, Apollo music and healing, and Aphrodite love. No God was all powerful and omnipotent. Judaism, of course, teaches that there is only One God who rules over all of the natural and supernatural aspects of the world. Only in the Land of Israel can a Jew fully experience holiness through nature as opposed to in the exile, where he can only experience the spiritual. Therefore, by remaining in exile the Jew is confining God's rule solely to the spiritual, which is akin to idolatry.

Although we are all outside of the Land of Israel we need to at least cultivate an understanding of and a yearning for the Land. In that vein I'd like to share with you some reflections from a recent MJE mission to Israel.

After landing at Ben Gurion Airport we headed up the coast on one of the main North – South highways. As I looked to my right, towards the east, I saw beautiful green hilltops. I realized that these were the hills of Samaria, located in what is commonly referred to as the West Bank. If the world, and a large part of the Jewish People, have their way these hills will one day be part of another country. It was then that the tiny size of the State of Israel became shockingly clear. At its narrowest point there are perhaps 10 miles separating a future Arab state from the Mediterranean Sea. My next thought was, "what are we doing here?" There are so many beautiful places on this planet where the Jewish People can settle and live peacefully. How about Long Island? California? Florida? We won't need an army to defend us from 100 million hostile enemies at our doorstep, and we can then concentrate on material success and the peaceful pursuit of happiness. Instead, we've chosen a tiny sliver of land with indefensible borders, no natural resources to speak of, and surrounded by millions sworn to our annihilation!

When we reached our first stop, Caesarea, I found an answer to my question. The modern day upscale town of Caesarea is built next to, and named after, an ancient city built by King Herod at the start of the first century of the Common Era. Although the ancient ruins of the palaces, stadiums, and sea port don't have much Jewish religious significance, they do testify to the fact that Jews populated and ruled the land for thousands of years. This is our connection to the land. It is our homeland. Our historical and national identity is located within its narrow borders. Outside of the Land we have no identity except that of stranger and wanderer. Only in the land can we connect to, and glory in, our past and find strength and stability for the future. Not in Long Island, LA, or Florida. Just in Israel. This is why we're there (in Israel).

A couple of days later we stood on a mountain in the Golan called Ben Tal overlooking the Syrian border and the scene of one of the most important battles ever fought in Jewish history. During the 1973 Yom Kippur War the Syrian army crossed the same border we were viewing with close to one thousand tanks. The only thing lying between this force and the cities of the Galilee were less than one hundred Israeli tanks. There was a point during the battle when only three Israeli tanks remained active. Despite their overwhelming power and advantage the Syrian army retreated. Despite the gallant bravery of the Israel soldiers there is no rational way to explain the events of the Golan battle. It was clearly a miracle. The Land of Israel is a land of miracles, a place where God is intimately involved with the destiny of the Jewish People. It is the only place where the Jews can defeat their enemies no matter how powerful or numerous they are. This is another reason why we are there.

While in the Golan, we went to visit the Golan Winery where we participated in a very informative tour of the operation. It is quite an operation. The ultra modern and spotless winery is almost entirely mechanized, and staffed by observant Jews. It annually produces millions of bottles of high quality wine. Many of the wines have won prizes in Europe and the US and are rated among the world's top tier vintages. What's most unusual about the Golan wines that surprises the world's expert vintners is that the small strip of land totaling no more than about twenty square miles is capable of producing dozens of different types of grapes that are ordinarily grown in different regions of France. Nowhere else in the world can the cabernet grape share such close proximity to the merlot and the chardonnay. This made a great impression on me. The Land of Israel is truly blessed with the potential to be bountiful. The produce of the land is first rate. Just taste the fruits, vegetables, dairy and bread products and you will recognize immediately that the Land is blessed. But it's not only the soil that is blessed. It's also the ingenuity and ambition of the inhabitants of the Land that is blessed. From agriculture to science and technology the Jews in the Land of Israel are achieving well beyond normal expectations. Israel is a place where a person can attain material success and live at the same standard of living as anyone in NY or LA. The skyscrapers of Tel Aviv, the industrial parks of the Galilee and Negev, and the vineyards of the Golan give testimony to the blessings of the Land. That's another reason why we're there.

Towards the end of our trip we went to the coastal city of Ashdod to visit the scribe who was writing the *Torah* scroll being donated to MJE. As we walked between the buildings in an apartment complex I could see only one thing: children. There were literally scores of little children playing in the walkways. They were all over the place! Everywhere I looked I saw Jewish children. The scribe, a Chasidic Jew in his late forties, and his very friendly and energetic wife, have fourteen children, five of which are already married with children of their own. Every family in the neighborhood most likely had a similar demographic. That explained the crowds of children playing outside. It was clear that the Land of Israel is not only blessed with agricultural bounty but it is also blessed to be the place that is ensuring Jewish continuing by producing our most precious commodity, children. These children can run and play freely in a safe environment where every stranger is really just another caring relative looking out for them. That's another reason why we're there.

After spending time in the north and the south of the country we finally made our way up to Jerusalem and proceeded to Mount Scopus for an overview of the city. It was a beautiful view, but the one landmark that stood out from the entire panorama was the golden Dome of the Rock, the mosque built about eight hundred years ago on the exact site where our holy temple once stood and will one day stand again. It made me feel a bit depressed. We've finally returned after 2000 years and we can't even have full control of our holiest place?

On Friday night we prayed the Kabbalat *Shabbat* service on a rooftop overlooking the Kotel plaza. It was incredibly inspiring to lead the prayers in that special place but then, as if on cue, the sound of the Muezzin calling the Moslem faithful to prayer filled the air. I once again noticed the domes of the two mosques perched on the Temple Mount overshadowing the Kotel and I once again felt depressed and deflated. The same people that look forward to our departure into the Mediterranean are dominating our holiest place. Then something happened. Jews began converging on the Kotel to pray. Many sang and danced. There was an overwhelming feeling of joy and peace. We too sang out loudly and the combination of all of our prayers filled the air of Jerusalem.

Our Arab cousins in the Middle East are consumed with destroying us. The terrorist groups lead by Hamas and Hezbollah have only one way of dealing with us: terror. Only hatred and violence flows out of Gaza, the West Bank, Lebanon, Syria, Iran, Iraq, and even some of the more so called "moderate" Arab countries. The Land of Israel, however, is a holy land. What does holiness mean? It means love and peace, not hatred and war. When I saw the Jewish People united in prayer on that Friday night, living in peace and striving to bring peace to their neighbors I knew that the Land would forever belong to us. When I looked at the domes once again I saw something completely different. Can you imagine there being a synagogue right in the middle of the holy area of Mecca? It's not even possible to dream about something like that! It would never be permitted and would be destroyed if it already existed, as is evident from history. But here, in our own country with a powerful army capable of destroying its enemies, we not only allow but protect and provide services to Moslem houses of worship on our holiest spot, the only one we have in the world. That is the ultimate show of love and peace and that is why we deserve and will always possess the Land of Israel, for only a people committed to love and peace can possess a holy land. Only in this holy land can we reach the highest levels of unity, brotherhood, and love. That's the main reason why we are there.

The most important thing that we can do, besides praying and supporting Israel, is to improve how we act towards our friends and community. We must treat everyone with caring and respect. The Talmud says that the Temple was destroyed because of baseless hatred, disrespect, and quarreling between Jews. The only way to correct that sin is to embrace our brothers and sisters with love and peace. If we do that we can be sure that this exile will end very soon and we will see the canopy of peace spread over Jerusalem, the Land of Israel, and the entire world.

ISRAEL VOLUNTEER MISSION
8/18/2006

I had the privilege of participating in a volunteer mission to Israel during the recent war against Hezbollah in Lebanon. There were about ninety participants on the mission, from young professionals to senior citizens, men and women, observant and non observant. We had two objectives: to physically help out in any way possible, and to show our support to the Israeli people. I'd like to share with you ome of the things I saw.

The first thing I have to say is that the Land of Israel is beautiful. However, to paraphrase the words of the scouts sent by the Jews in the wilderness to spy the land, it is full of giants. At first, we felt like grasshoppers in their presence. By the end of the trip, that changed.

The first task I took part in was helping run a day camp in Maaleh Adumim, near Jerusalem, for children whose families lived in the north. To avoid spending their days and nights in bomb shelters under fire, these families decided to travel south. Without relatives or friends able to accommodate them, they ended up staying in temporary housing in Maaleh Adumim. The real giants of this story are the men and women who opened up their town and facilities to "strangers", running activities for their children, providing them with food and in many cases clothing, but most of all, treating them not like strangers, but like family. There are no refugees in Israel, just family.

The following day we traveled south to Sderot. Sderot is a so called "development" town right near the Gaza border which has been the primary target of hundreds of Kassam rockets fired from Gaza. Several people have been killed by these rockets which have also caused significant damage to houses, schools, and roads. The most significant damage however, other than the deaths and injuries, has been psychological. According to the deputy mayor the people of Sderot, especially the children, are living under unbearably strained conditions knowing that at any moment the sirens can announce incoming rockets with only about ten seconds of warning. How are the people dealing with this? Are they running away? No. In fact, they are beginning to subdivide lots for new homes on the outskirts of town right near the Gaza border. The people of Sderot are not giving in to the enemy. They are standing strong and proud.

We stopped our buses at a street corner where a kassam had once fallen, and I took out my guitar and started to play and sing a fast tune. Everyone joined in and we began dancing. We also brought out a huge duffle bag filled with toys. Suddenly, cars began to stop, and children began converging on us. As their parents looked on with teary smiles their children got their toys and experienced the joy that normal children are supposed to experience. It was a truly heartwarming moment. A little while later we left Sderot, but the children stayed on with their parents. Many of them undoubtedly dreamt of sirens and rockets that night. These are the giants of Sderot.

The next day we finally had the opportunity to travel up north. Our first stop was at an army base in the Golan where we met a group of soldiers who had just returned from a three week mission in Lebanon. These tankists were nineteen and twenty years old. Most of them looked like boys and were polite, gentle, and in good spirits. Perhaps only a year or two ago they were boys. But now they had faced the enemy and seen death and destruction, protecting their people. Now they were giants. Some were from America, South Africa, and Russia. Each one was motivated and proud of what they were doing and prepared to go back to Lebanon if ordered to. They were very touched to know that Jews from America cared about them and supported them, and we in turn were touched that we could give them strength and purpose. These giants were our little brothers. How could we possibly not be there for them?

Next we traveled to Kiryat Shemona, right on the Lebanese border. We visited the Hesder Yeshivah overlooking the city from where we could see some of the areas that were hit by the nearly one thousand missiles that fell there. The Yeshiva stayed open throughout the war and the students, those who were not in the army, spent day and night helping the majority of the residents who stayed while the missiles fell. There were miraculously, no deaths from missiles in Kiryat Shemonah but there was destruction, terror, and tremendous economic hardship. Despite all of this the residents were optimistic. There was no depression, just hope and hard work in Kiryat Shemonah. The same was true of the entire north. These giants are used to being under fire, and they don't give up.

The following day I had the privilege of volunteering to package rations at a large army base near Tel Aviv. Our group of ninety was divided into two warehouses, where we lined the conveyor belts and packaged food in boxes that we then stacked and helped load onto forklifts for removal into storage. We worked alongside young male and female soldiers from the four corners of the world. At first they really didn't understand why we had come there, but they were grateful for our hard work in any case. The officer in charge of our warehouse thanked us for our much needed help, specifically for packing rations for 9000 soldiers. He then told us how touched he was that we chose to come and help. They were all very touched. It finally hit home. These giants need us. They don't see us as grasshoppers, but rather as brothers and sisters.

We're all one family. We're all responsible for each other. Just because we don't actually live in Israel doesn't mean we're not responsible for our family members who do. We are responsible. Everyone reading this is obligated to help the family in some way. A great way is to actually go there and help out in any way possible, or at the very least, to help strengthen the economy, that has been greatly weakened by the month long war, by spending money. If we can't actually go at this time, there are many funds and organizations collecting much needed money that we can contribute to.

I have a confession. When I first heard about this mission I wasn't sure if I should go. It wasn't that I was scared. I simply wondered whether my presence would actually make a difference to the people of Israel. I decided that I could make a difference and that it was important for me to show my support. Everyone on the mission made that same decision. We had to do whatever we could, no matter how trivial. We all came to Israel as grasshoppers wanting to help the giants there. While there, we realized that there were no giants and grasshoppers, just brothers and sisters. They needed us as much as we needed them. We all became partners in the same journey, members of the same family. No more them and us. Just one family, forever.

EPILOGUE – DESTINY

I read a very interesting story in a book by Po Bronson called, "What Should I Do With My Life?" There was a young Tibetan man, raised in a refugee camp in India, who was graduating from an Indian university but didn't have much hope in finding a successful and fulfilling career. Besides the obvious strikes against him as a refugee in a country not his own, he simply didn't know what his destiny or calling was. That is, until one day he received a letter, signed by the Dalai Llama, informing him that he was the reincarnation of an ancient Tibetan spiritual leader whose territory encompassed the northern region of Tibet. This was his destiny. He went to one of the main monasteries of the religion and studied there for twelve years, and took his place as a revered spiritual leader of thousands.

Wouldn't it be great if we could each get a letter informing us of our own destiny? How much clearer and more fulfilled would our lives be?

The truth is that every Jew has that letter. It's called the *Torah*. It informs us that we are the descendants of a very ancient and holy people who have striven towards spirituality and holiness using the special instructions given to them by God in the *Torah*.

The *Torah* doesn't tell us what career to choose, or where exactly to live, but it does give us the guidelines to lead a fulfilling life in harmony with our destiny. All we have to do is study those holy words and find our own personal path – our destiny – within it.

CPSIA information can be obtained
at www.ICGtesting.com
Printed in the USA
LVOW07s1612171117
556704LV00003B/281/P

9 781438 263984